THE STORIES OF U.S.

THE STORIES OF U.S.

A COLLECTION OF STORIES OF UNDOCUMENTED AND FIRST-GENERATION IMMIGRANTS LIVING IN AMERICA TODAY

SAHERISH S. SURANI

NEW DEGREE PRESS

COPYRIGHT © 2019 SAHERISH S. SURANI

All rights reserved.

THE STORIES OF U.S.

A collection of stories of undocumented and first-generation immigrants living in America today

ISBN   978-1-64137-358-6   *Paperback*
       978-1-64137-696-9   *Ebook*

CONTENTS

PREFACE	11
NOTE FROM AUTHOR	17
AURY	31
PABLITO - PART 1	51
EMILY	69
SAHARA	83
DONAVAN AND PAOLA	113
KABIRA	133
PABLITO - PART 2	151
IRIS	173
AKINA AND AIDEE	191
EPILOGUE	205
RESOURCES/NEXT STEPS	209
ACKNOWLEDGMENTS	217

"There's really no such thing as the 'voiceless.' There are only the deliberately silenced, or the preferably unheard."

—ARUNDHATI ROY

PREFACE

This book recollects the stories of only ten, of many million, undocumented and first-generation immigrants living in the United States today. However, these stories are not the only ones, and they are not a typecast of any and all stories. Each story is unique in its own way, containing aspects that may seem far more intricate and complex than anything you have ever experienced, while also encapsulating events and emotions that mirror many of your own.

This is a book for those who have not seen their own stories shared enough, for the ones who are courageous enough to speak out and voice their own journeys, and for those who are willing to hear the stories of those who have too often been silenced, too often feared for their lives, and too often been tokenized for something that they are not.

To those who were willing and brave enough to share their stories with me, and for the many who live through it every day; to the ones who never give up and face battle after battle; to the undocumented, to the first-generation, to the immigrants—thank you for braving the unknown.

All parts of this book are based on true stories. All names and identifying features have been anonymized to protect the privacy of the individuals who have shared their stores.

"The fact of storytelling hints at a fundamental human unease, hints at human imperfection. Where there is perfection there is no story to tell."

—BEN OKRI

NOTE FROM AUTHOR

The city of Corpus Christi, Texas, is home to the popular fast-food chain Whataburger, Latina popstar and singer Selena Quintanilla, me, and an estimated 27,315 immigrants, of which around 9,400 are undocumented.

The immigrants in Corpus Christi have contributed to the diversity of the community, an aspect of the culture that many of the locals take pride in. According to a report by the South Texas Economic Development Center of Texas A&M Corpus Christi, more than one in three Texans speak a language other than English at home, with the largest numbers being Spanish, Vietnamese, and Chinese. Mirroring trends that can be observed across the rest of the United States, immigrants in Corpus Christi tend to be younger, with 75 percent of them being of working age (as opposed to only 50 percent in the local native population), *meaning that they are more likely to contribute to local taxes and help stimulate the local economy.*[1]

* * *

I rolled up the windows of the car, the salty ocean breeze leaving my hair in a knotted mess. The sunset was still just barely visible as I drove over the bridge heading back into the city. I'm not quite sure if I hate Texas summers for all the heat, humidity, and mosquitos it brings, or if I'm in forever awe of its warm sunrises and sunsets.

Sitting in the back seat, my sisters argued over who had the gooiest cookies in town, while my parents talked to each other over and around them. Somehow, I am always the designated family driver. Even after years of my driving, my dad insisted on sitting in the passenger seat beside me, obnoxiously clutching the door handle when I drove even a mile over the speed limit.

On this particular summer night, I felt at ease. My older sister, Sara, was home from college for a couple weeks before setting off to do research in Peru. My little sister, Zoya, was excitedly getting ready to start her first year of college, while I had just finished mine. Going to college for my sisters and I hadn't felt

---

[1] Lee, Jim. "Immigrants in Corpus Christi." Economic Pulse. Texas A&M University Corpus Christi South Texas Development Center, 2017. http://stedc.tamucc.edu/files/Econ_Pulse_2017_10.pdf.

like a question; it was just part of the plan. College had been a dream for my parents. Long before they knew each other, both had immigrated to the United States from Pakistan, ending up on opposite coasts—my mom on the West and my dad on the East. Immigrating to America in the early 1990s was a different story for them than the reality of what many individuals face today. While it was by no means easy to get accepted to an American university or obtain a student visa, it was even harder to finally decide to leave everything they knew behind: family, friends, places, language, and the communities that had raised them.

That summer night, we had gone out to dinner as a family, celebrating my grandpa's birthday at the most authentic fish and chips restaurant that the city of Corpus Christi had to offer, newly reopened after sustaining damage from being directly in the path of Hurricane Harvey the previous fall.

After we spontaneously decided to pick up dessert, I pulled into a parking spot at the restaurant. I turned the headlights of my car off to keep from blinding the young gentlemen standing near the front of the car in the night, which had become dark so quickly. My sisters ran in to get the pizookies (pizza-shaped cookies and ice cream— what could be better?).

They scurried back to the car, clicked in their seatbelts, and I put the car into drive and flicked my turn signal to home.

Before I could even change the radio—just seconds after pulling onto the road—a flash of light illuminated the car and I was nearly blinded by red and blue flashing lights in the rearview mirror behind me.

Panic immediately set in.

I was being pulled over by a police officer, and a fear crept over me at what might happen, much like millions of others like me who also have brown skin in America.

* * *

Over 10.7 million people live in the United States as undocumented immigrants.

While many believe that undocumented immigration should cease to exist because citizenship to the United States can be obtained through a visa process, it is imperative to understand that documentation isn't that easy.

The United States' immigration waitlist has over four million people, while there are another 150 million people who would emigrate from their countries to the United States if given the opportunity to do so. Today's media coverage of immigration under the Trump administration has relied heavily on illegal immigration and often reports on the uptick of undocumented individuals. But contrary to those reports, undocumented immigration has been declining by as much as half in the last ten years, according to an article by Peter Beinart of *The Atlantic*.

Most live most days in fear: fear of being caught, fear of losing everything they worked to build in a new country, fear of being deported, and fear of losing their families. A small mistake like forgetting to turn their headlights on could radically change their lives for the worse. Furthermore, of the 10.7 million undocumented immigrants living in the United States, less than sixty-five thousand of them graduate from high school, and less than 10 percent of these students even continue on to college because of the systematic barriers that make it difficult to do so.

What separates me from those 10.7 million people?

I am a *legal* citizen.

* * *

My headlights. They were still off.

How had I forgotten to turn them back on? My sweaty palms clasped the steering wheel tighter. My dad turned the radio off. My mom and sisters went quiet. I put my turn signal on once again and pulled over into the closest parking lot.

I tried to stay calm.

As he took the insurance papers out of the glove compartment, my dad reassured me and told me everything would be okay. My mom chimed in to apologize. I took my license out of my wallet. I rolled my window down and greeted the officer good evening, trying to steady my voice. He informed me of what I already knew: my headlights were off. I watched as the officer visually scanned the inside of my car, starting with my dad and I in the front seat before looking to the back seat.

He took my insurance and license and returned to his vehicle.

No one said anything.

When he came back, he told me that because I didn't have any prior infractions on my record, he would let me go, and a sigh of relief escaped me. I put my documents back in their rightful places, turned my headlights on, flicked my turn signal, then merged onto the road.

As I drove home, I couldn't help but wonder why I had been so scared. My entire family was in the car with me. I wasn't speeding. I didn't get into an accident. While, technically, yes, I wasn't following the law, I wasn't doing anything glaringly illegal. My parents, and both of my driving-capable sisters, could have made the same mistake I did. My mom and dad wouldn't have been mad had I been issued a ticket because they were there with me.

What I did was careless and could have been avoided, but it was a mistake.

Even to this day, I think about what would have happened if we didn't have car insurance?

What would have happened if I didn't have a license?

What would have happened if I didn't have a *valid* license?

What if I wasn't a citizen of the United States?

What if I, or anyone else in the car, was undocumented?

A small mistake such as mine could have resulted in much more than a mark on a record or a ticket for many families in my city. A small mistake such as mine could have ended the life that so many people worked so hard to build. Something like forgetting to turn your headlights on can cost many families their entire livelihoods. It can result in deportation.

I got lucky.

* * *

I am lucky my parents immigrated to this country when they did. I am lucky they did so long before having me and my sisters. I am lucky to be a United States citizen. But I didn't earn this right like my parents, who waited for years and years to be approved for green cards and eventually citizenship. I just got lucky.

But others have not been so lucky—particularly those 10.7 million undocumented immigrants. Instead of being handed citizenship like I was, many of these people have worked far harder and far longer for the same privilege I was handed.

According to Quorum, a public affairs software platform, just eleven years ago, in 2008, there were a mere 874 mentions of the word "immigration" by federal officials in social media posts. That number has dramatically risen: in 2018, there were over 47,970 mentions of immigration. As of June 2019, there were already over 25,000 mentions of it. Additionally, the conversation around immigration has largely been driven by Democrats, constituting 58.3 percent of all mentions of immigration, while Republicans trailed behind with 41.1 percent. Furthermore, since 1989, there have been 6,952 bills that have been introduced (as of June 2019) into Congress that have mentioned immigration.

However, it is important to note that even though almost *half* of our elected officials talk about immigration, and almost seven thousand bills have been introduced, very little has been accomplished to progress this conversation on a legislative front. This is not an issue that will be automatically resolved over time, or an issue that has made significant strides of progress. Instead, the reality is that the legislative aspect of immigration has faced decades of stalemate and puffery.

This is not an issue that will go away on its own.

Living in the political climate of the United States today, with an administration that often puts the politics of issues before the humanity of them, the stories of undocumented individuals are vital to our livelihoods. First-generation Americans and immigrants are often tokenized by the mass media for the worse. Because of this, I wanted to share the stories of a series of individuals—who not only live in our communities, but help them thrive—and the ones who must overcome immense barriers to achieve the same amount of success many of us are privileged enough to not even realize we have.

* * *

Through exploring the intersection of immigration and politics, I began to understand the gravity of why these stories are so important. Hopefully, a pending cultural and social shift in the America we know today will occur where politics and simply being human can actually intersect. Immigration isn't a simple concept. It's political. It's emotional. It's complicated. But it is an issue that, at its core, is a human rights issue. Unless we try to understand it now and hear these stories today, we will never be able to learn from each other.

These are the stories of humans who are stronger than I am, more resilient than I am, more determined than I am, and more deserving than I am. These are the stories of undocumented mothers and daughters, husbands and wives, brothers and sons, teachers and doctors, students and artists living in America today.

These are the stories of us.

"You may not control all the events that happen to you, but you can decide not to be reduced by them."

—MAYA ANGELOU

AURY

The ringing school bell brings me back to reality. I slip out from the metal chair connected to a wooden desk. Grabbing my *mochila* from under my chair, I shove my books into it, and sling the bag over my shoulder.

As I make my way into the chaotic hallway, an amalgamation of scents instantly washes over me. Chicken nuggets? Lasagna? Mystery meat? I'm not sure what will be on the lunch menu today, but I am most definitely sure that it won't be as tasty as the food from back home.

I dodge a group of kids circled around some lockers. I slip past the hallway assistant trying her very best to guide kids into the cafeteria. I duck under a group of student council officers hanging up a banner for next week's spirit week. I deftly avoid Mr. Simonsen and his attempts to get more kids to sign up for the eco-club. Finally, I make it to the third door in the last hallway, Mrs. Mosey's.

I take out the Tupperware box with the sandwich I made for myself this morning. I replaced my backpack for the fabric and pin cushion in the cubicle marked "Aury." Taking my materials, I settle down in front of a sewing machine.

"Aury, you're going to spend another lunch period working on your dress?"

"Hola—hey, Mrs. Mosey. I enjoy sewing and working on my project."

"Well, alright, honey. It's coming along really well. Let me know if you need anything at all."

Mrs. Mosey's presence alone was a calm within the storm of high school. Her classroom, lined with needles and thread, was my haven. It reminded me of home. It was a mental escape from Mr. Simonsen's calculus lessons, which often seemed more foreign to me than English.

In Mrs. Mosey's classroom, I was in control. I didn't have to think so hard about mentally translating my thoughts from Spanish to English. I didn't have to think about my parents working so hard. I didn't have to think about how I couldn't control Mamá's immigration status. I didn't have to think about my brother still in the Dominican Republic. I didn't have to think.

I could just sew.

From one project to the next, one dress to the next, I could make what I wanted inside the walls of Mrs. Mosey's classroom. The gentle whir of the machine as I pressed down on the pedal was the only language I had to understand as I sat behind it, watching the spool unwind and the presser foot bob up and down against the fabric.

Mamá had taught me how to sew on her machine when I was much younger. I would sit at the kitchen table, my foot barely long enough to reach the pedal. She would leave the windowpane propped open halfway during the summer days to let the salty ocean breeze in to cool the house. With the beach a couple miles away, we would spend almost every weekend there. My cousins would bring the food to grill, and my mom always took care of the snacks, meticulously packing diced and seasoned cubes of watermelon and guava in separate containers.

As soon as the sand and waves were close enough to see from the back of our small station wagon, all of us would be giddy.

Antonio, my older cousin, would start to pull on his yellow and blue swim flippers, elbowing me in the gut as he fumbled to do so. I would shove him back, and before I knew it, both my cousins, Antonio and Ralfi, would put their weight against me, pushing me into the window of the back seat. Mamá would tell us to settle down with no avail.

The car would pull to a stop and all of us would pile out of the car, one on top of each other, Antonio falling out in his too-large flippers, Ralfi with his pool floaties already on, and me, with one flip-flop on and the other somewhere on the floor of the back seat. My toes would touch the burning asphalt, and I'd run to find relief in the coolness of the sand.

Mamá would run after me, pleading me to come back for sunscreen. Antonio and Ralfi would come from behind me and push me into the sand, starting to bury me almost immediately. I'd call out for Mamá's help as they covered my face with sand, their small hands shoveling the hot sand from cracked plastic cups from home.

Soon enough, my cousins would get tired of tormenting me and run to the waves. I'd follow them, eager to keep up. Walking toward the water, I'd feel the sand turn from individual grains to mush before I couldn't even feel it anymore. My head would bob as I tried to remember to doggy paddle to stay afloat. The saltwater getting into my mouth, making me gag. Batting my eyes to keep the salty water out, a combination of it and tears would stream down my face before becoming one with the waves again.

Mamá would call out to us from where she and *mis tíos* set up the cookout. Running out of the cold water, my hair dripping and tangled, I'd run to the towel she held out for me. "*Mija, come la comida primero.*" She would slap my hand away as I reached for a mango paleta, almost melted in the hot sun. I'd settle and pick up a cube of watermelon instead, the red juice dripping down my chin as my tío plated fried fish for us.

For as far as my eyes could see, the beach was lined with a combination of vendors and small tents like ours. This beach was different from the others. It was ours. There weren't white beach chairs filled with tourists and their floppy sun hats embroidered with Pinterest quotes.

Our beach was local. The vendors caught the fish and fried it in front of our eyes. There were small flies swarming around the Popsicle stands. There was loud music blasting from each of the different tents. This beach was noisy. But it was ours.

Sitting here in Mrs. Mosey's class, those are the moments I miss the most. I miss the calmness within the chaos. In the States, sure it's loud and chaotic, but it's loud and chaotic in a language that I have trouble understanding. Mrs. Mosey speaks no

Spanish, yet is somehow the only one at school who understands me. She reminds me a bit of who Mamá was back home: strong, independent, and confident. Now, she is gone before I get up during the week and most evenings when I get home; she is rushing out the door for her second job but always sure to plant a kiss on my forehead before leaving. On weekends, I can hear Mamá making herself a cup of black coffee long before the sun rises. When I wake up, she's bent over the kitchen table, poring over study materials for her citizenship test.

Recently, Mamá's busy days don't begin and end with work. Instead, they've been muddied by the bureaucratic tangles my school has been creating. As one of the few students in the English as a Second Language class, Mr. Cinnter, for some reason unbeknownst to me, has singled me out as the student farthest behind. It also could be possible that Mr. Cinnter isn't the biggest fan of me because I might roll my eyes or deeply sigh every time he opens his mouth to speak, which is almost always because he speaks so ignorantly. Almost every day, he passes off comments in English under his breath about how people should have to learn English before coming to the United States or how if we knew we were going to move, why didn't we "bother learning the language first"? Well, to be frank, I am not a big fan of Mr. Cinnter either.

The others in my ESL class are incredibly sweet but have been living in the States for most of their grade school experience, so their English is by far much better than mine. Esmeralda even sneaks me the answers to the crossword puzzle exercises we do. I mean, how am I supposed to know that 12 across is "isthmus," when I don't even know what that word is in English or Spanish!

Mr. Cinnter sent my academic advising team an email about how he feels that I am not improving in my English speaking skills (which is clearly false. Just ask Mrs. Mosey!) and thinks that they should explore the possibility of holding me back an additional year and looking at the option of me graduating next year. Since that email, my counselor, Dr. Sherwood, has been on me to have a meeting with my parents. Every time he says my *parents*, I always clarify that it's just my mom, but he really doesn't seem to get it.

Dr. Sherwood is a nice man but seems to be a little too stubborn in his own ways. All of last week, he kept calling my teachers during class to tell them to remind me to tell my mom to email him back. I didn't really know how to tell him that we don't pay for Wi-Fi, so she wouldn't be able to reply until she went to the public library. I don't even know how Mamá has the patience or energy to somehow make everything work. She never complains, and even when I know she's beyond exhausted, she always sits down to ask me how school and friends are going. Mamá has always encouraged me gently.

"Buen trabajo, mija."

Her faith in me was enough to make me believe that I could do anything, even start over in a brand-new country with her when I was just thirteen years old.

When Mamá and I immigrated to the United States of America, neither of us could speak English. We left behind our friends and our family: all the names, faces, and places that we knew.

I look up from behind my sewing machine. The room is filled with other members of the sewing club coming in to work on their projects, gearing up for competition in two weeks.

Caroline and Riswald walk in together arguing about a TV show being dropped for the next season. Caroline is working on an apron for her grandmother. A couple weeks ago she made the oven mitts to match. Caroline talks a lot, in the best way. Most of the other students exchange pleasantries with me but don't bother trying to have a full conversation. Caroline just keeps talking. To be completely honest, I really don't understand half the things that she says, but it's nice that she doesn't treat me any different than the others. Riswald isn't actually sewing anything. He's knitting a pair of gamer gloves to wear when he plays video games. He can never remember what direction he was working in before and undoes a quarter of his loops before realizing he is knitting the wrong way. At this rate, hopefully he'll have one glove by the end of the year.

Mrs. Mosey catches our attention as the others settle into chairs. She pulls up the daily announcement emails from one of the assistant principals and starts to read them off. "Next week is 'Red Ribbon Drug Free Week' spirit week. Monday is 'Lei Off the Drugs,' so wear Hawaiian-themed apparel; Tuesday is 'Team Up against Drugs,' so wear team jerseys or attire; Wednesday is…" The persistent ringing of her desk phone cuts her off.

She looks up, a little worried, and scans the room, looking for a particular student. I sink into the metal frame of the desk chair, hoping it isn't me. Her eyes meet mine and she gives me a half smile while nodding to whoever she is speaking to, letting out a few "mhmms" and "okay, I see" while she does. After she hangs up the phone, she looks at me and says, "Aury, sweetie, Dr. Sherwood is with your mom in his office, and they want you to go down there and talk."

"Oh, okay. I'll go now, yeah?" I ask while starting to wind the spool of thread.

"Yeah, go now, honey. Don't worry about cleaning up; you can do that when you come back."

I nervously bite my nails while Mrs. Mosey puts the phone down. Catching myself in the act, I move my hands away from my mouth. Mamá hates when I bite my nails. My stomach churns, and I can feel the toast I had for breakfast making my stomach feel unsettled. No one likes being called to the front office, but especially not me. Ever since we moved to the United States, I've tried to blend in, to make it easier to assimilate to the culture so that no one asks Mamá or I more questions than we can answer. And being called to the front office is the easiest way to stand out.

Unsure whether to take my stuff with me, I tidy up my desk space but eventually decide to leave all my stuff behind. Mrs. Mosey picks up right where she left off in the middle of her announcement spiel. The classroom quiets from the buzz of chatter and side conversations as she speaks.

The hallways aren't exactly quiet while class is in session, but they aren't noisy either. The sounds of students chatting within the classroom walls seem to echo and bounce off the metal lockers lining the hallways. My heart sinks further and further down as I pass each classroom. What could Dr. Sherwood be talking to Mamá about right now? She's missing work for this.

I take the second right at the end of the hallway and turn into the office. Wiping my sweaty palms on the legs of my pants, I swing open the heavy wooden door. Mrs. Catalina greets me and says that Dr. Sherwood is expecting me. I've been to his office a handful of times but can never seem to remember exactly where it is. I guess it shows in my expression because Mrs. Catalina says, "The door on the left, right after the conference room," gesturing toward it.

I can hear Dr. Sherwood's voice as soon as I approach his office, even though his door is almost shut. His office door is covered in post-it notes, thank-you letters, and graduation cards from his old students. Will he put my graduation card up too? I lightly knock on the door, unsure whether I should just walk in or wait for him to open it. He hollers for me to come in, and I carefully open the door, knowing there is a chair right behind it, likely where Mamá is sitting. Careful not to knock any of the picture frames on the wall over, I take a seat in the other chair across from him. I've never understood why counselors are given office space to accommodate a single person, when their job literally requires them to have multiple people come into their office.

Dr. Sherwood's office is an organized clutter. He has a large whiteboard calendar right next to his desk, which is shoved into a corner of the room with an organized assortment of EXPO markers magnetically stuck to it. It's easy to tell exactly where he writes because there's an arm's length smudge left in its place. The desk itself is covered in picture frames of all sizes and colors. There's one of his daughter as a toddler crying in a mall Santa's lap. Another picture of his daughter, his wife, and himself dressed in white shirts and blue jeans in front of a brown studio background. There's also one of Dr. Sherwood dressed in navy and black graduation regalia accepting a diploma, for what I presume to be his PhD.

His office smells like candles, but I can't exactly put my finger on the scent—it's musky but smells a bit like damp laundry at the same time. The single overhead yellow ceiling light doesn't help make the office seem any bigger than it actually is either. Dr. Sherwood's desk is piled with manila folders, each overflowing and spilling with an assortment of papers. I recognize the pink, blue, and yellow choice sheets we had to fill out before the beginning of each year to pick up the classes we wanted to enroll in during the semester. On top of the hundreds of papers that cover his desk, Dr. Sherwood's working space is littered with loose staples and paperclips. It is truly a wonder how he can find anything.

Mamá squeezes my hand as Dr. Sherwood greets me. "Aury, I was just discussing with your mother your progress throughout the school year. I spoke to Mr. Cinnter, and we think it would be a good to explore the idea of the possibility of you staying for one more year and then graduating next year."

I knew this was exactly what Mr. Cinnter told Dr. Sherwood, but his words make me angry. "What do you mean? I am speaking very good English now, I am doing well in my classes, and am even participating in extracurricular activities. I don't understand why I couldn't graduate this year like we have been planning since I first started school in New Jersey." My blood starts to boil at the thought of staying another year surrounded by students who think I don't speak any English and teachers who refuse to acknowledge that it's my second language. I look to Mamá, my eyes pleading for help.

"I know this must come across as disappointing news, but really, it will aid in a much smoother transition to college if you decide to go."

"I already applied to universities; I am just waiting to hear back. Why wouldn't I go to college? What do you mean?"

"Well, I just want you to know that going to college is not the only decision, and it is not always the right decision, especially for students, like yourself, in different circumstances."

"Different circumstances? I'm not sure I follow." I didn't know what Dr. Sherwood was trying to imply. Different circumstances as in poor? As in immigrant? As in with a single, undocumented mother? As in because English wasn't my first language?

"Well, I just mean that your situation isn't the same as many of the students here. That's all. Really. I just don't want you to be too upset if you don't get into the colleges that you applied to. It might be better to prepare for another year and try applying again."

I have the grades and the extracurricular activities. My letters of recommendation were very strong. I submitted my applications way before the deadline. Why wouldn't I get into any of the colleges I applied to?

"Dr. Sherwood, with all due respect, I don't think it's necessary for me to repeat senior year. I also don't think it makes sense to even discuss this possibility, if you are so worried about me getting rejected from all the schools I applied to, before those decisions even come out. I really appreciate you speaking to Mr. Cinnter and checking up on my progress, but I don't understand why we are discussing this so early into the school year."

"Aury, I can understand why you are upset, and I completely agree. We can wait to make this decision in a couple months once you hear back from these colleges. I just wanted to speak to both of you earlier rather than later to make sure we didn't run out of options or time."

Dr. Sherwood turns to my Mamá. "Please take your time and consider all the options. I am here for you and want the best for both you and Aury. It was a pleasure to meet you."

With that, I grab my backpack and thank Dr. Sherwood for his time. Mamá follows suit, and he opens the door of his office to escort us out. He guides us to the main hallway door before thanking us and turning back to head to his office.

Mamá squeezes my shoulders, "*Te veré en casa, bien?*"

"Sí, Mamá. I'll see you at home tonight."

"*Todo estará bien. Te amo, mi amor,*" she says as she hugs me again.

"I know it'll all be okay. I love you too, Mamá." I turn and head down the hallway back to Mrs. Mosey's class. The same sounds of students excitedly shouting inside the classroom are just annoying now. Why are they so happy? Because they are legal citizens? Because they learned to speak English before they could even use the restroom on their own? It isn't fair that I'm being punished for something I never had control over.

My blood boils as I play the conversation we just had with Dr. Sherwood over and over again. I didn't choose to be born in the Dominican Republic. I didn't choose to move to the United States. I didn't choose to leave all my primos behind. I didn't choose to leave the beach behind. I didn't choose to come to a country where the beach is littered with plastic bags and shards of beer bottles. I didn't choose any of this. I miss not speaking English. I miss carefree Mamá. I miss the salty smell of the sea. I miss home. I let the tears stream down my face. Why bother wiping each one away when I know another one will follow?

Upon entering the classroom, I realize that the last class period has ended and a new one has begun in its place. New faces that I barely recognize are now in the same spots where Caroline and Riswald were sitting moments ago. Using the end of my sleeve, I dab my puffy, red face. Remains of skin-colored makeup and the sharp black lines of my mascara stain the soft fabric. Folding the sleeves inside, I slide my planner into my backpack and start to clean up my space. I feel the heat from the eyes of twenty strangers in the room staring. I dab my face again, but I'm sure it is quite evident that I was crying.

I carefully remove my dress from where it's bound under the presser foot, cut the thread, and lay it across the desk. My hands quiver as I gently fix the pins and fold the fabric, careful not to prick myself. Taking all my materials to my designated cubby, I go back to the desk for the sewing machine. I pick up the pedal and wind the cord around it, making sure not to leave it in tangles for the next person who uses it. Mrs. Mosey, seeing me struggle with the machine, comes over to help me carry the machine to its docking station. Patting my back gently, she tells me it's all going to be okay. I don't doubt her, but I don't entirely believe her either.

* * *

Migration from the Dominican Republic to the United States was largely instigated after rebel forces killed Rafael Trujillo, the Dominican dictator, in 1961, causing civil unrest and a fear for safety. US intervention, in hopes of aiding the economic and political instability during the transition period, accelerated the emigration movement out of the Dominican Republic.

The Dominican immigrant community has contributed largely to the economic stability, atmosphere, and cuisine of many major cities' microneighborhoods, such as Washington Heights in New York City.[2]

---

[2] Zong, Jie, Jeanne Batalova Jie Zong, and Jeanne Batalova. "Dominican Immigrants in the United States." migrationpolicy.org. Migration Policy Institute, May 3, 2019. https://www.migrationpolicy.org/article/dominican-immigrants-united-states.

> "We're all under the same sky and walk the same earth; we're alive together during the same moment."
>
> —MAXINE HONG KINGSTON

PABLITO
PART 1

January 13th

It's been a while since I've journaled. But I've had so many thoughts and so much going on that I didn't really know where to stop. There was a mental health presentation in school today. I guess the teachers and stuff think it's important with like the college application process and everything like that coming up.

They told us that we need to start opening up before we start to drown, and I think I should probably do that because right now I feel like I'm tired of doggy paddling, but what else can I do when I don't know how to swim? I don't want to drown.

What would Cara and Penelope and Sebastian do then? I don't even want to think about it.

Wait, actually, isn't this the point of journaling? To think about things? Maybe I should be thinking about these things. I don't want to stay in this town for college, and I know that I can get into a state school, maybe even get some scholarships or at least a loan to cover the cost.

But what about the sibs? Cara isn't even in preschool yet, so I don't know who would drop her off and pick her up from day care. Sebastian still won't be able to even get his learner's permit for another two years, and he's starting high school next year, which is enough of a headache on its own. I know Penelope would try to help, but I mean, there's only so much a fourth grader can do. She should be working on meeting her reading goals every week instead of changing Cara's diaper.

It's just really annoying being the oldest. Obviously, it's not something anyone can control, but it's not fair that Sebastian gets to do whatever he wants and hang out with his friends and stuff. Like yeah, I want him to be able to have that, and he's younger and he deserves to have fun, but I'm always the one who gets stuck with doing everything around the house.

I don't feel like my siblings are my siblings; they feel more like my kids. And I didn't sign up for that. I mean, yeah, I know, Ma and Pa work hard and that this is only happening because they're working hard for us. I mean, Ma has like three jobs and Pa works offshore, so it's not like he's really even around to help. And I feel bad that Ma has to work so much, but my job refereeing for soccer tournaments doesn't pay a lot, and I mean, it's also only on the weekends. I really want to look for another, more real, job, but I think it would have to be something very early in the morning so that I can get the kids ready for their school but before my school starts.

Job ideas:

- Holiday Inn front desk receptionist/bellboy/kitchen help
- CVS retail associate
- UPS package handler
- Home Depot cashier
- FedEx customer service helper

January 14th

We had another session about the college application process, and I don't even know where to begin. I have so many questions. I know that applying is hard and that actually getting in is even harder, but I also think that because Ma and Pa don't have papers that could make it even worse for me. I shouldn't say things like that or even think them. I mean, it doesn't make things worse for me. They came so that we could have better opportunities.

Honestly, I can't even imagine what it was like for them to come here. I don't think I could leave home for another country where the people spoke a completely different language on the off chance that I would be able to stay. Or, I guess, not be allowed to stay but stay secretly anyway.

You know, the funny thing is, sometimes I forget they don't have papers. I still remember when they told me that they were here illegally. It was the field trip in fourth grade to go to the Valley. They said that we would have to bring identification because even though it was still in Texas, we might have to cross the checkpoint. I wanted Ma to be a chaperone so bad. Because of all her jobs, she had never really become a classroom mom or come for any of the functions and holiday parties and stuff. But I remember when she said that she wouldn't do it, first saying that it was because she couldn't take off work and then after I kept nagging, she broke down into tears.

I think that's the only time I've ever actually seen her cry. I didn't understand her pain then, but I think I understand it a little better now because I truly don't think I could ever understand it completely. I mean, at that time, it was just me and Sebastian. She couldn't come to any of my choir concerts or science fairs or history plays, rites of passage in elementary school. And then I begged her to come to this one activity, which was literally the one thing that she would never be able to do. It's too much of a risk to try to mess with border patrol or the checkpoints or police officers.

That one trip could have literally been the end of the life that I had always known, life in America, and not just for me, but we could have been separated as a family—Ma and Pa being deported and Sebastian and I being put in foster care or who knows what. There could've been the chance that there would be no Cara or Penelope. I can't possibly think of all the repercussions (this is me trying to use the SAT words in real life so that I can actually learn them) that could have occurred from a single decision.

I think it's pretty wild that literally every single decision has this mad power to change the entire course of the world that we live in. I watched *Interstellar* (I think that this will probably be one of my top favorite movies of literally all time) in my physics class last week and since have been thinking about this thing called chaos theory.

And I've been thinking about it a lot, and I really do think that every possible outcome of a decision exists and that maybe they just don't exist on this planet or in this universe, but I mean, there must be other universes and other...I don't even know what to call it, but other things or lives or versions of lives that exist in which the other outcome exists.

I think there is a universe out there when Ma said yes and came on the field trip with me, maybe one where we didn't even get stopped at the checkpoint and another one where we did. There is probably a universe in which Ma and Pa never came to the US and maybe even one in which they didn't get married or even meet, and one, or many, I guess, that don't have me in them.

My thoughts are getting quite all over the place, so I think I should head to bed soon. I'm going to take Penelope to get a new white shirt for her uniform from Goodwill after school before I have to pick up Sebastian from soccer practice, so I should probably get some good rest tonight. So, I guess, with that I bid you adieu (another SAT word!!) until tomorrow.

January 18th

It's been a crazy last couple of days. The day that I was supposed to take Penelope to get a new shirt, she ended up getting the flu. We're actually not even sure if it is the flu, but apparently she was coughing at school and didn't look too well, so her teacher sent her to the nurse. And the nurse was scared that it was the flu, so she wanted her to go to the doctor, or really, she wanted her to go home so that other kids wouldn't get sick.

There were only two hours left until school was over for that day, but they still called Ma to come pick her up. She asked if Penelope could stay in the nurse's office until school ended because she couldn't just leave work, but they insisted she come immediately.

Well, by the time she got there and everything, it was almost time for school to be over. So it was this huge deal when really it shouldn't have been. The nurse told Ma to take Penelope to the doctor the next day, but we still don't really have health insurance and stuff so Penelope just stayed home. She was still coughing and tired and stuff, but it didn't really seem like that big of a deal.

I did my homework in her and Cara's room until late that night so Ma could go back to work. But Cara was also being really whiny, I think it's probably because we weren't giving her enough attention. And it was making me annoyed when she was crying because I couldn't concentrate on my calculus worksheet, so I asked Sebastian if he could take Cara to Ma's room so that Penelope could sleep. But then Sebastian started yelling at me and said that he needed his sleep too because he had a soccer tournament the next day.

We ended up yelling pretty loudly, which only made Cara cry more and Penelope wake up. I felt so bad, so I told Sebastian to go to sleep and then I rocked Cara until she passed out too. After I finished the parts of my math homework that I understood, I went to change the towel on Penelope's head, and she was really burning up. I was so scared. I wanted to wake Sebastian up but really didn't want to get into it again with him, and I knew I couldn't call Ma because I didn't want to disturb her at work.

I put a wet towel on Penelope and took off all the blankets, but man, I had never felt anything so hot. I decided just to sleep on the floor next to their bed that night, and it's so good that I did. I'm not sure at exactly what time, but Penelope started to throw up. I carried her to the bathroom because I really didn't want Cara to get sick too. It took a long while for her to calm down because she was crying and saying that the vomit was burning her throat.

I made her some tea to soothe it before she went back to sleep. The next morning, Ma came home, but I told her that I would stay home from school that day to stay with Penelope. There was no way that she was going to be allowed to go to school in her condition, and if Ma misses work last minute, she could easily get fired. Ma took care of Penelope while I ran to walk Cara to day care and Sebastian to school. He was still as angsty as ever about the night before.

I am definitely not looking forward to his high school attitude. Penelope got better throughout the day and then it was the weekend, so it's good that she had the chance to rest fully. And, I mean, it's also good that the weekend came right in time because if it didn't, I still don't think they would have allowed her to go back to school.

Also, a small job update! My friend Carl said that he knows that there is a local grocery store that is hiring for unpackers and stockers in the morning. He's going to apply too. Carl has his own car, so he said he can take me with him when he goes. I really hope that this job comes through, I mean, we could really use the money. If Penelope gets sick again, I think we would definitely have to take her to the doctor, and we all know that there's no way we can afford that right now.

January 19th

Hello, Journal!!

Ma was able to leave work a little early today to pick up the kids from school. This was great news because I was able to go with Carl to HEB, the grocery store I mentioned before, to apply for a job. It was a lot more paperwork than I thought it would be, but I filled all of it out and submitted my application. I also talked to the onsite manager, Christi, who was really sweet. She said that I would find out about the status of my application by the end of the week.

I really hope I get this job. I mean, it is actually perfect for me. I can work early mornings before getting the kids ready for school. And it won't interfere with me having to be home after school to help them and get ready for bed. Other kids at school who work at HEB were also telling me that it's a great place to work because they are very understanding for students about hours and stuff. It would be so ideal if I got this job. I'm keeping my fingers crossed, and it would be great if you could too, or, I guess, keep your spiral crossed because journals don't have hands.

January 20th

I'm getting a little anxious because I really want the job, but patience is a virtue, apparently. So, I guess I'll just keep waiting.

Penelope is feeling much better, which is really good. I am also so happy that Sebastian and Cara are feeling okay too. It would've been such a mess if one of them caught whatever Penelope had.

School is good. I mean, as good as it can be. I have a calculus test tomorrow, so I guess I should probably go study all those derivative rules now instead of continuing to write. Write in you after my (hopefully aced) calculus test!!

January 21st

My calculus test went really well, I think. I hope. I remembered the rules of the product, sum, difference, and quotient rules for derivatives. So, let's just hope that I applied them correctly. I actually really like math. It doesn't always make sense to me, but it makes sense. I am not sure how to put it into words properly, but, I mean, even if I don't understand it at the moment, I know that if I study hard enough and focus well, that I will be able to understand it. English and history and science aren't really like that.

In biology, we're doing Punnett squares. We use them to figure out the genotypes that two individuals, or plants, or really any species, can produce. And, I mean, they're pretty straightforward when there's only four boxes, but when there's twenty-five or thirty-six squares because there are more traits to compare, it becomes too confusing. There are too many ways to get the right answer and too many ways to be in the wrong.

In history, we're learning about the War of 1812, which is interesting and all, but I'm pretty sure I don't want to dedicate the rest of my life to spewing out facts about it—like how Francis Scott Key wrote the words to "The Star-Spangled Banner," which didn't actually become the national anthem until 1931, at the Battle of Fort McHenry or how the final battle of the war actually took place after the treaty to resolve it was already signed. Because I don't feel particularly connected to the history of America, it feels like I'm just memorizing and regurgitating information rather than actually learning it.

I think this may also be because my relationship with America seems a little complicated and murky right now. I mean, it is a great country, at least my parents thought so when they immigrated. But it's frustrating to me how Ma and Pa have to almost live in hiding. It makes me question if it's even worth it, you know, to live in a country that has all this opportunity if you can't access that opportunity. I know what Ma's answer would be: of course it's worth living in hiding because that means the kids and I can have all these doors open to us.

But ever since I've been learning more about applying to college, I've learned that yes, there are all these doors, but some people waltz through them, not knowing that there was ever a chance that door wouldn't be open, while others (like me and Sebastian and Cara and Penelope) will likely have to bang on that door and find ways to get it to open. And even then, we might not be able to walk through it.

I am a little stressed about applying to college. I really want to talk to Ma and Pa about it. Pa comes home for four days next week before having to leave to work on the oil rig at sea again. I guess I could talk to them about it then. But the thing is, I don't really want to. When Pa comes home, it is always so fun. We always go out to eat lunch and sometimes even to the beach or something. I think he makes sure we have extra fun when he's here so Cara and Penelope, and I guess even Sebastian, don't grow up resenting him for being gone for so much of their lives. I know that he works hard and that he does it for us, so I would never even think about not forgiving him for the recitals and concerts and tournaments of mine he misses.

Ma and Pa live for us, so we can't be upset with them for things like this.

January 22nd

Still no call from the grocery store. :(

January 23rd

I hope they call with an application update, or I think I will actually lose my mind.

January 24th

We didn't have school today because it was a teacher workday. For teachers, it's a normal school day, just without the students—so, I guess, not very normal at all. In the morning, I made breakfast for the kids. I tried making pancakes for the first time and must admit, they could have been better. I thought that after I put the mixture on the skillet, they would shrink. But turns out, they come out pretty much the same size as they went on. So we had a couple very large, slightly burnt pancakes. But all of us just drenched them in syrup, so it wasn't as bad as it could have been.

After breakfast, I turned on an old cartoon movie to keep Cara occupied. I helped Penelope with her Valentine's Day box. Every kid in their class has to decorate and bring their own box, and then everyone brings valentines for all the kids in the class. There is a prize for who has the best box. I don't think Penelope will win, but she had a lot of fun making it, which is what matters. That reminds me, I need to go buy the candy for her class's valentines.

I also helped Sebastian a little, well, as much as I could, with his English essay. I helped him edit it and everything, but it's based on the book *To Kill A Mockingbird*. I've never read it before, so I couldn't help him that much with the content, but I tried as best I could.

Sebastian promised to watch Cara and Penelope so that I could stop by the grocery store with Carl to ask for an application update. Christi, the manager, wasn't there, so we still don't know what the status of our applications is. I am very over this whole "waiting" thing. I just want to know. Yeah, I really want this job, but if I don't get it, it's not the end of the world at all. I just want to know so that I can apply to other places.

Applications, applications!!! There are just so many. I have decided that I will talk to Ma and Pa about college when he comes home tomorrow. I really think it's important for me to have this conversation with them so that I can start narrowing down where I want to apply, like if out of state would even be an option (which I really don't think it would be), public or private (although I'm pretty sure private will not be possible, even with scholarships, most are just too expensive), and ultimately if I can even go out of the city and to a university. Community colleges are much cheaper, but the thing is, I want more than just an associate's, and I want to experience life on my own as a typical college student. I'm going to write down the talking points I want to cover with them before actually sitting down and discussing the idea of college with them face-to-face.

"We realize the importance of our voices only when we are silenced."

—MALALA YOUSAFZAI

EMILY

Immigration from China to the United States has been characterized by two waves, the first arriving in the mid-1800s and the second beginning in the late 1970s. The first wave of immigrants consisted primarily of Chinese males coming temporarily to satisfy the need for cheap labor in the United States. However, the Chinese Exclusion Act of 1882 prevented legal Chinese immigration to the United States.

The second wave of Chinese migration to the United States, as a result of the United States' 1965 Immigration Act and the state of US–China relations in 1979, consisted primarily of white-collar workers and university students, creating barriers to legal entry pathways for many of the Chinese working class.[3]

---

3   Zong, Jie, Jeanne Batalova Jie Zong, and Jeanne Batalova. "Chinese Immigrants in the United States." migrationpolicy.org. Migration Policy Institute, June 13, 2018. https://www.migrationpolicy.org/article/chinese-immigrants-united-states.

* * *

A cup of frozen mango chunks
...so I put in three-fourths
Two handfuls of strawberries
...so I put in one
One and a half bananas
...so I put in one and a fourth
A cup of milk
...so I put in two
Half a scoop of ice
...so I put in three

Bà always tells me to save fruit
I think the customers are on to us
"Why is this smoothie so watery"
"It doesn't even taste like there are mangos"
But he says that they'll keep coming back
in his broken English, of course

Every day is the same
Wake up
Shower until the water turns cold
Eat a piece of toast
Pack one for lunch
Walk to the bus stop
Sit in the back

Take a spitball out of my hair
Get asked why I'm wearing the same
shirt from yesterday
Keep walking
Try not to react
Get books from locker
Realize I didn't finish homework
Go to bathroom
Splash water on face
Sit in the back of class
Get pushed in the hallway
Go to bathroom
Eat toast in the stall
Fail math test
Get on the bus
Listen to music
Walk home
Change into uniform
Walk to Bà's store
Make smoothies
Get yelled at by customers
Cry in the freezer area
Watch the sunset from inside
Help Bà clean up
Walk home together
Eat dinner together but silently
Start homework

Fall asleep before finishing it
Repeat

The teacher passes out the invitations
Everyone is giddy with excitement
I open the envelope
Awards Ceremony: May 8th at 11 a.m.
The middle of the work day
Of course
Everyone is chatting
The girls behind me giggle
The guys in front of me shout
Everyone's parents will come
Except mine
Of course

There was a loud knock on the door
The whole house rattled
I ran to Bà's room
He told me to do what we practiced
My palms sweat
He hides in the bathroom closet
I go to the door
Inhale
Exhale
Inhale
Exhale

I open the door
"Hello, Officer. Is everything okay?"
He asks if my parents are home
He asks if Li Zhao is there
"Yes, that's my father. But he isn't home now"
He looks past my shoulder into the house
"I think he is running some errands"
He asks when he will be back
"I'm not exactly sure, Officer"
He asks how old I am
"Sixteen, but seventeen next week"
I smile
He doesn't smile back
He sees through my lie,
knowing I'm not as old as I say I am
He says he'll come by later
"Okay, Officer"
He walks away down the path
looking back at the house again
I close the door
Leaning back
Breathing
Tears streaming
This isn't the first time
I am here legally
Bà isn't
They've come to the smoothie shop

They've come to our home
Will they come to school next?

There are letters shoved into our door
Right where the metal meets the wood
One falls to the floor
PSAT Prep Classes Info Session
I kick it under the doormat
We're only in middle school
But counselors ask about college
They ask about majors
They tell us about test scores
They make us sign up for exams
But we're only in middle school
I asked Bà if I was going to college
He sighed deeply
Looked stressed
His gray hairs are starting to show
And said not to think about it
Because I'm only in middle school

I unplug the OPEN sign in the window
Locking the door
Drawing the blinds shut
There's an aggressive knock on the door
I look at him and shrug my shoulders
Pointing to the closed sign

He mouths "It'll be quick"
I sigh
Unlocking the door to let him in
He scans the menu with his eyes
I put my apron back on
He asks for a strawberry banana smoothie
Easy enough
And a large mango blitz
Alright
And two Caribbean breezes
Okay
And a small strawberry kiwi
I thought it was going to be quick
He takes a seat and I get started
Chopping fruit
Pouring milk
Adding ice
He's talking on the phone
His feet are up on the table
I blend it together
Pour it in a cup
Add a lid
And grab a straw
Five smoothies later
I ring him up
He's still on the phone
"Sir, your order is ready"

He hands me his card
Without looking at the total
Still talking on the phone
He signs the receipt
He doesn't look at the amount
He doesn't add a tip
You're welcome for your smoothies, sir

Geometry
Spanish
English
and Science
All these classes to take
But I don't feel like I'm learning
Actually, maybe I am learning
Learning how to hide my tears
Learning how to take spitballs out of my hair
Learning how not to get caught eating lunch in the bathroom
Learning how to sink in my seat so the teacher won't notice me
Learning how to blend in
Learning how to go unnoticed
Learning how to be invisible

Bà is put together
His shirts are always pressed
His fingernails are cut short
His face is kept clean-shaven

But
His pants are missing a button, although unnoticeable
His shoes have holes that are carefully patched
His jacket has threads that are only getting looser
Yet
His hair grays
His tired eyes show
His face sags
Bà is falling apart

I wake up as if it's any other day
But it's not
I'm 16 now
But no driver's license for me
But no big party for me
But no cake or gifts for me
It's September 15th
I don't even think Bà will remember
A small newspaper-wrapped box sits on the kitchen table
His scrawny handwriting shows it's for me
Tearing the paper apart, I open the box
A rusted locket
Inside is a picture of Mà
and baby me
I snap it shut
Opening my drawer of pajamas, I bury it
Mà doesn't deserve to be a part of my birthday

She left 14 years ago
She can't come back now
Not even a picture of her
This is my day
This is my September 15th

"Our histories cling to us. We are shaped by where we come from."

—CHIMAMANDA NGOZI ADICHIE

SAHARA

---

15 September

My dearest Mosley,

It doesn't feel like I've been in America for three weeks already. Three weeks since I last saw you. Everything about this country is so different from home. But before I talk about America, I must tell you about the airplane.

Mosley, it is like nothing I have ever imagined before. The airplanes are not nearly as small as they would look like when we would stand on the beach and clap as they passed over our heads. These are much bigger than the trains, even. After you left the airport, I went through so many security checks.

They check everything. The machine beeped when my bag went through, so they had to take it out and look at it separately. The security agent took out my biltong because she said that meats weren't allowed. I put some in the big suitcase and it was still there when I unpacked it, so that's good. But after I went through all the security, there were so many shops and so many restaurants. I really didn't even think I was still in South Africa. If I could describe it, I think I would say it was like the V&A Waterfront, but even better.

I walked into one store, and I thought everything would be so cheap because they didn't have that many things in the store. But there were four security guards standing in just this one store! I don't understand why they were guarding maybe five or six bags and a couple pairs of shoes. It was a very nice store, though. There was even an expensive carpet in just this one store.

I walked around a little and then found a spot by the gate station that my flight was assigned to. I made sure that I had my flight ticket, memorizing the number 44B, to make sure that I wouldn't forget my seat number when I finally got on the airplane. After two hours of waiting, they called on us using the speaker system to line up by boarding group. This is another one of the numbers that is printed on our flight tickets. Group 1 gets to board first, and Group 5 boards last. I was in Group 5, so I waited until they called for us.

After scanning my ticket, I went through a long glass tunnel to the entrance of the plane. There was a line even here because it was taking a while for everyone to actually find their seats and get settled. It's a good thing that I knew exactly what my seat number was. There were many different seats on the plane. The first section were very nice. The seats were very large. Each one was like the recliner sofa in Kwanele's house. There was even a big pillow and warm blanket at each of these seats. My seat was a bit smaller. There were three seats on each side of the plane in my section. I had the seat in the middle.

The woman who sat by the window in my row had flown many times before. She gave me some great tips. She told me that I should try to stay awake at least until they came around with snacks and drinks. The gentleman who sat on the other side of me, near the aisle of the plane, did not like flying at all. He spent the better part of the flight hunched over a small paper bag. His elbows also kept crossing over the hand rest into my seat, jutting into my stomach and waking me up from my naps. But I decided not to say anything. I didn't want to make him feel any worse.

The flight attendants were very nice. There was even a little button you could push at any time during the flight, and they would come and bring you whatever you needed. I never pushed the button, even when I was so thirsty for a glass of water. I just didn't want to disturb them.

As cool as it would be to travel the world, waking up in new places every day, and getting paid, I don't think I could ever be a flight attendant. First off, I don't have the patience. Some of the passengers were very annoying. The lady behind me in 45B said that there was too much ice in her cup and then complained when her drink wasn't cold enough! The audacity!

I also think that it would be too much traveling for me. How would I know where home is? How would I know what it feels like if I never stayed in a place long enough to make friends or meet people? I think for me, home isn't a place. It's the people.

Sorry for getting a bit off track, Mosely, but anyway, the airplane. I think my favorite part wasn't the free munchies or the TVs that had so many shows (Mosely, there were sooo many shows and movies and songs—truly anything your heart could desire was preloaded on these screens); it was the takeoff and landing.

I was a little nervous the first time we took off; it reminded me of the time the tour company you worked for gave us that free bungee jumping pass. It felt kind of like jumping off that bridge. Up until the edge, you feel very nervous and sick. But the closer you get to the edge, the more carefree you feel. The plane was the same way. I felt like I was going to throw up my breakfast as it sped up faster and faster. But it was a different kind of fast. I didn't feel like I was going to fall out of my seat, only that I was going to pee my pants. It's a good thing I didn't. Imagine how embarrassing that would have been!

And finally, when the wheels of the large bird were no longer on the ground, I felt weightless. I could feel everyone on the plane take a deep breath of relief. We were in the air. All of us. All on the same plane. We all had the same fate. It was strangely comforting. The landing brought with it a similar feeling of eerie comfort. We were safe.

I don't really like thinking this, but part of me knows that we are probably much more safe in the sky than we are on the ground on this Earth. I've tried to keep all my preconceptions of America at bay, but I can't help thinking about my safety, and the safety of our future, when I hear of all these shootings in colleges. That's where I am going to be: in a college. What if there is a shooting? I know, I know that they happened back home, but at least there, we knew what areas were safe and which areas to avoid.

But here, in America, I don't think that even the "safe" zones are "safe." If a school, even one with young kids, isn't safe, then why would any place be?

I am just now realizing that I haven't even begun to tell you about my school or about my life here. I must go now; there are so many meetings that I have to keep attending. This one now is with a mental health advisor. She is supposed to make sure that I am adjusting well. I don't think this kind of occupation exists in South Africa. Maybe one day. I think it's very helpful and important. Anyways, I must go now but will write to you again soon.

Love you always,

Sahara

* * *

13 October

My dearest Mosely,

I am keeping true to my promise and even though so much has happened since the last letter I wrote you, I want to catch up on the things I did not get to tell you first. But before any of that, I must tell you how much I miss you.

Some days I wake up and forget that I am in America now. I go to roll off of the sleeping mat just like back at home only to realize that now I sleep on a raised bed. I have almost fallen off many times, but catch myself just in time.

I miss spending time sitting with you after dinner. Our plates still on the table. What we think will be just catching up on our day turns into watching the sun set and then the sun rise. Every two hours, I would tell you that we should get ready for bed, but somehow those two hours turn into two more and then two more. I miss talking to you about family and technology and politics and religion.

Really, I just miss talking to you. To hear your voice again, I would do anything. I miss watching that sparkle in your eye when you talked about your future, our future. I miss seeing your brow furrow when you were thinking about a question you didn't have the answer to just yet. I miss watching you think, knowing your mind is moving much faster than your lips could ever convey.

I miss you, Mosely.

It won't be long until college is over and I can come home to you, or maybe, just maybe, you can come to me.

Speaking of college, it is by no means easy. And I'm not even talking about the classes because while those are quite difficult, it is the people and the rules and the unspoken social rules that I have been having the most trouble with. My English has definitely gotten much better, even in just these few weeks. I mean, no one speaks Afrikaans, so it's not like I would be understood if I did. And people are far more accepting of my broken English than I would have thought. While many people scoff me off when I raise my hand in class or ask a question at the library help desk, I think there are many more who are actually willing to listen and who actually want to hear what I have to say.

I am taking this one class about how gentrification affects different cities, even Milwaukee. Three weeks ago, I didn't even know what gentrification was or that it is a word. My politics professor would definitely explain it better, but it is pretty much what happens when an outside group comes and renovates lower income or lower class neighborhoods to make them better. Yes, it sounds great. But I've learned what happens is that the renovations make it much more expensive, which means that the people who were originally living there usually can't even afford to stay. So they get kicked out of their own homes.

This makes me wonder if something like this is happening in Muizenberg. I mean, we see more and more tourists. And the beach side has restaurants that serve food that isn't even authentic South African cuisine, like the fish and chips stall or the sushi restaurant.

I really think that gentrification is happening in that area. It is beautiful, but is becoming too expensive. I can't even remember the last time we went, and it is almost like our backyard. Actually, I do remember. It was when we went to Tiger's Milk for Ozarie's birthday celebration. I remember getting the chicken tacos. They were very yummy. And you got the malva for dessert. That was also very good. Food here just isn't as good as it is at home

Okay, I promise I will stop comparing everything to South Africa soon because I am trying to "live in the moment," as they say here, but home food just tasted so much more real and fresh, even when there was less of it.

That is one thing I must say I love about America: the portions. I don't understand how anyone could go hungry here. There is food everywhere and so much of it. Buying it in the stores is very expensive, so I try to spend minimally when I go. But they have food banks and food pantries, even on our university's campus, where you can go and they give you food for free, like a donation.

They also have these thrift stores that sell clothes and other things, like kitchen appliances, for much cheaper than at the store. They are a little used, but what does it matter? I saw this one dress I really liked. It was black and simple. I was going to purchase it, but don't have it in my heart to spend that much money on an item of such luxury. It was twelve dollars, which is almost 170 rands! Maybe if I get invited to somewhere nice I will go and splurge on it, that is, if it's even still there.

I feel like in these letters all I do is talk and talk and rant. But it is a little nice, yeah. I feel like there are things that I could tell you here, in these letters, that I could never tell anyone else. Everything I say, it doesn't matter in what language—English or Afrikaans—or where, whether that is here—in America, or in South Africa—I feel like I have to think about so carefully. You know me. And you know that I don't really care about what others think about me. But the thing is, I think I do.

Being here, I've learned that I really don't know who I am. I think so much about what others will think of what questions I ask in class, what clothes I wear to the even the library, and just who I am, generally. But I don't understand why I care. I don't know these people, and these people definitely, definitely do not know me.

We are strangers. While, yes, some of them are becoming acquaintances and friends, why do I care what the other complete and absolute strangers think of me? This is something I have been thinking a lot about the past few days. I know that it doesn't matter, but then why do I dress up for other people or think so hard before I raise my hand, often waiting so long that I miss the opportunity altogether?

I hope you are getting these letters. I will try to save some coins and send them in my next one so that you can write and post a letter back to me. My heart stays waiting to hear from you.

Love you always,

Sahara

* * *

19 November

To my dearest Mosley,

Keeping true to my promises, I have included in this envelope a prepaid return envelope. It will be a bit folded and probably creased, but the nice gentleman at the post office assured me that it wouldn't be a problem for you to send it back.

Since my last letter, things have once again changed quite a bit, namely the weather. When I first came here, I was already a bit confused. I mean, it was August and the weather was pleasant, even more than pleasant, actually, it was nice. It was warm. Back home I was leaving the rainy winter, and here, I had arrived at the end of summer and the beginning of autumn.

But now, winter has come. And this winter is not anything like a Muizenberg winter. There is snow. So much snow. I don't even think the top of Table Mountain or Lion's Head gets this much snow.

The first snowfall was so beautiful. I sat in my dormitory room all day, just watching it fall through the mesh-netted windows. I woke up when the greenish brown grass was just barely visible beneath the cloud of white. The trees went from brown and bare to dusted in white.

I stepped away from the window to make myself lunch, and when I returned, I couldn't tell that it was the same view I had left just minutes ago. I felt like I was living inside one of the snow globes they sold at Checkers in the holiday aisle. It was just as magical as it is in the movies. Even more magical, though, because it was *real*.

If it were a movie, I think there would have been a warm fire running and a cup of hot chocolate brewing. But because it wasn't, it was just me in a pile of blankets because turning the heat on is too expensive to afford right now, and a pile of reading waiting to be done for class the next day.

I did allow myself enough of a break to go and just feel the snow outside. It smelled clean and homey, even though our home has never smelt of such. I waited on the steps as the flakes fell on my outstretched palms and on my hair, and really, on everywhere.

One of many things that that day taught me was that snow is very deceiving. Covering my hair, making me look like I had a bad case of dandruff, I thought I would be able to just dust it off. But that was, in fact, far from the truth. When it hit my hair and my sweater, it was not at all what it looks like. It looks soft and lovely but acts like rain—making everything wet and soppy.

But even aside from that, my first snowfall was breathtaking. I wish I could say every day of snow since has been just as magical and beautiful, but that is also far from the truth. The day after the first snowfall, when I woke up for class, the beautiful white cotton-candy layer that was covering the earth had already been tainted brown.

Walking out into the weather to class, I learned how snow just continues to deceive. It wasn't soft and fluffy like it had been the day before, but slippery and slick. I felt my feet give out from under me on my first steps and then slowed down and had to consciously think about every step from then on. Day after day, the snow on the ground transformed into slippy, sluggish, brown mush. Gross.

But be it or not, the weather could be worse. Everything could always be worse. Life is hard, but life is good. I always catch myself complaining about small things here and there, like how "beef jerky" is kind of like biltong, but really, it's nothing like biltong. While biltong is the perfect combination of dry yet chewy, I have found that beef jerky comes in two different styles—either too dry or too chewy.

I am trying to keep a tally of how often I complain so that I can minimize it. I guess I should add one for today because of that biltong statement. I think, in America, and not just for me, but even the other students around me, it is so easy to forget how lucky we are. Other students complain about the smallest things, like when the line is too long in the cafeteria or when the classroom theater is a bit too cold or a bit too warm. And don't get me wrong, I find myself also complaining about these things.

But why? These worries are so meaningless, and there are so many bigger things to complain about and so many other things to think about.

I mean, I still can't believe that I am here, in America, 14,000 kilometers from home, from you.

Even more so, I can't believe that there are people and donors and organizations who were willing to take a chance on me to let me come and study here. They believed that I could be more than just a township girl, and I really feel like it's my responsibility to take that weight, to take the scholarships they're giving me, to take the information I am learning and make something out of it, make something out of myself.

I really have no idea where I am headed or what I will do with my life, but I know that I will become something because I really don't think I can't not.

I will talk to you soon, Mosley. Hopefully you will be able to write back, but if it is not possible or safe enough to get it to the post, please do not worry.

Love you always,

Sahara

* * *

10 January

To my dearest Mosley,

I hope you and everyone else are doing well. I miss Mum and Dad and all your little siblings as well. I hope Mikayla is getting excited for the summer play, and I can only imagine how giddy the triplets must be for the surfing summer camp. I remember how you would tell me that they were envious of Olwethu because they weren't old enough to go yet.

The waves must be crazy huge this time of the year, yeah? I still remember the first time you took me out on the waves. I think I ended up with more water in my mouth than there was left in the ocean. The huge waves must mean that there are hundreds of surfers lining the beach. Hopefully this means that business is good.

Another thing I have thinking about a lot since my one politics class last semester, I think I told you a little about it and how we learned about gentrification, is tourism and the effects that it has on local businesses. I think it must be very frustrating for you now, and probably always has been but I don't think I really ever pressed you on your thoughts about this, about selling your carefully crafted wallets and bracelets to all these tourists.

I think it is still beautiful. I mean, your work is extraordinary and anyone would be foolish not to want it. But does pressing images of the Big Five and the lions and the tigers and the outline of Africa feel…a little like you're selling out your work? I don't mean that in any way but the best. You are so skilled and so brilliant. And the world deserves to see your work, and at least in this way, it is. And it frustrates me how these tourists that come don't always see your work for how exquisite it is, unless it is stamped with something that they can take back home to show off as a souvenir of their worldly travels. But then again, as you would say, "Business is business."

My darling Mosley, I cannot wait for the days when we can both do what we love without having to worry about bringing home food to our families. That day may seem very far off for you, but I don't think it is as far as we believe. Good times are coming, my love, I just know it.

I have told you about the weather and the food here, but I haven't really gotten the chance to tell you about the people. I have made some very close friends these past four months (can you believe it has already been four months??). One of them is my hallmate, Katrina.

In ways, I feel like she is both a sister and a mother to me. She has been living in the Midwest in America all her life, and I promise you, she has the best tips and tricks like it's nobody's business. She used this spray on my shoes that helps in the snow. I don't have the perfect snow shoes, so I have been wearing the sneakers (the ones we bought together at Checkers). Before this spray, they would get very wet and drenched in the snow, but now they fare up much better than before. It's kind of like a repellent but for the fabric.

Katrina has also taken me under her wing a bit. She is a year older but lives in this dormitory building because her housing plans fell through too late. She tells me the quietest places to study on the university campus and how to sneak food out of the dining halls in Tupperware (I must also tell you all about this later! They are these small clear plastic boxes with colored lids that are made for storing food so it doesn't go bad as quickly). Katrina is genuinely one of the nicest people I have ever met.

A few weeks ago, I was very stressed about an assignment for a literature class I am taking. We had to write a twelve-page analysis comparing two of the readings from the first couple weeks of school. It was our midterm paper, so it is worth more than just a regular assignment.

That is also another thing I don't really understand about this school system. In almost all of my classes, I have two "midterm" papers or exams, but in none of these classes do these assignments actually happen in the middle of the term. And the fact that there are multiple "midterm" assignments kind of takes away from the fact that it is supposed to be a "midterm" assignment, no? Why not just call it a triterm paper or exam?

Well, anyway, back to this midterm paper. I was so stressed that I wasn't going to finish on time that I cried. A lot. I was even more stressed because here you don't write essays on paper and turn them in to the teacher like we did back home. You have to type it on these fancy computers using word processing software.

It took me a very long time to get used to it. I still type very slow, but I am learning. I found this helpful website that has practices on how to type faster, so maybe I will go on there and use it when I don't have as much homework.

Well, anyway, because we have to type all our essays on this fancy software, I can't even do it in my dormitory. I have to go to the library, which has a computer room. They call it a computer lab, but really it is just a room full of maybe 30 or 40 computers. When I first got to the university last fall, they gave me a username and password, and this is what I use to access the software on these computers.

Many students have portable versions of these computers, or laptops, and they carry them around everywhere they go. Laptops really do make it easy to work from anywhere, but they are wildly expensive. Carlos, another one of my friends who also receives scholarships, told me that at the beginning of each year, there is a special fund that students receiving financial aid can apply to to receive things like laptops and even the fancy word processing software to put on them, for free. So, I will definitely be looking into that later.

Back to the paper, I was worried sick that I wouldn't finish and that would mean that I would do badly in the class and then lose my scholarships and would, inevitably, fail (which I now realize is a very spiraling out of control way of thinking, but that is what was going through my head). Katrina calmed me down and stayed up with me all night while I did the paper. She worked on her own assignments while I did research for mine and then wrote it. But I know that she didn't have to stay up doing it because none of her work was due right away. Her company in that time was more support than I could have ever asked for.

It's funny, actually. Between the library and my dormitory, I feel weirdly comfortable in a place that is so foreign in so many ways to me. I mean, I still get shaken up when I see so many cars on the road, and even more so when they stop at the crosswalk to wait for students to cross the road.

The green road signs in English still catch me off guard, and every time I see the American flag flying so high above, I have to take a moment to catch my breath. I'm not sure exactly what it is, but that flag reminds me that I am so far from home, that I am in a land that I never imagined I would have the opportunity to come to, much less study in.

Today, when Katrina asked me where I was going, I found myself referring to my dormitory as home. It's been making me wonder what home is. My room is a haven, but it is by no means anything like home. Home is where my people are. Home, to me, is where you are.

Mosley, every time I walk by past my mailbox, I peek in to see if there is anything there. When there is an envelope, my day is always made better just on the chance that it is from you. I miss you so much, Mosley. There isn't a day, probably not even an hour, that passes when I don't think of you.

Love you always,

Sahara

* * *

4 March

To my dearest Mosley,

I don't know how I'll find the words to write this letter. I truly don't think I will ever be capable of finding the right words to express how much I love you and how much I miss you.

It's been two months since Kwanele phoned with the news, and I wasn't able to sit down and write this last letter to you since then. Even now, I am not sure I will be able to say goodbye. I don't think I can ever say goodbye to you because you are such a large part of me. Saying goodbye to you would be setting a big part of myself to rest as well.

To say my heart is heavy would be a complete and utter understatement. It is absolutely broken.

Since his phone call, I have been walking around in a trance. Without you in this world, I feel like the sun rising each day is just taunting me, and I cry as it sets because that marks another day without you.

When Kwanele called, I thought it would be you using his tele. Never in a million years did I think that he would be phoning to tell me about your sudden passing. I couldn't breathe when he told me. I couldn't believe what he was saying to be true. I didn't want to believe it.

How is it that you, the nicest, most pure soul, would be the one to be caught in the crossfires of the Capricorn violence? You have never been cruel to this world, so why is it being so cruel to you?

I didn't understand. I couldn't understand. I mean, I still don't understand. And I don't think I will ever be able to.

I do think that the world works in mysterious ways, but for me, this is an unforgivable sin on the universe's part. You deserve to live more than anyone else because you are the reason there is a will to live, for me.

I wanted to come for your burial ceremony. More than anything, I wanted to be there to say goodbye and to help lay you to rest—it is the least you deserved. I couldn't save enough in time, and I know that you would have wanted me to use that money for school. You would have scoffed at the idea of spending 30,000 rands. I could hear you telling me that you would always be with me, and I feel that. I have felt your presence with me so many times these past two months.

You are my strength, Mosley.

My Mosley, there's a million and one things that I miss about you and a trillion more that I love about you.

I miss sharing a piece of chocolate cake with you from the Xpressions café on the first Sunday of every month. I miss walking along the beach, feeling the sand beneath my toes, just waiting for the sunrise, with your hand intertwined in mine. I miss hiding from the surfer kids in the colored houses just behind the playground as you would chase them around until they were giddily laughing and completely exhausted. I miss you getting fresh biltong from Kwanele, which was supposed to last for a whole month, at the first weekend of the month's market, and then hearing you complain for the next three weeks about how there is no more biltong left in the house. I miss watching you spill the warm maple syrup that came with the chicken strips on your shirt at the Blue Bird Garage on Fridays. I even miss letting you convince me into taking the shortcut to Checker's by crossing the train tracks, even though one of us was bound to trip on them one time or another.

While I miss you immensely, I love you even more.

I love the sparkle in your eyes when you talk about something you love, or talked, I suppose. I love how you would chase around your siblings until they sat down to do their homework. I love how you would always convince me to wake up early to watch the sun rise and how you would drag me outside to watch it set. I love how you, more than anyone I have ever met, understood the value of the world, how you saw the best in people, even when it was hard, and how you never, ever gave up.

My love for you only continues to grow. I hope to see the world through your eyes—carefree, optimistic, and completely and utterly beautiful. You will forever be my love, my life, and my strength, Mosley. I love you, always.

Love you eternally,

Sahara

***

It is estimated that at least two people die as a result of vigilante or group attacks every single day in South Africa.

The township that Mosley and Sahara are from, Capricorn, is one of the oldest and poorest settlements in the Western Cape. While there has been no official census, the local Council has estimated there to be around eight thousand people living in the township, half who speak Afrikaans and half who speak Xhosa.

The land on which Capricorn is built belonged to the Council, giving the current residents no official rights to the land or resources.[4] Under the apartheid government, many were forcibly deported to other parts of South Africa, while others left due to constant harassment. However, the people of Capricorn persisted, rebuilding their homes at night when the government would tear them down during the day.

For many years, Capricorn had no electricity or piped water, an issue that is of constant worry even today. The shacks that residents live in are constructed from a variety of materials, whatever they can find, usually pieces of wood and tin. These homes do not provide adequate shelter from heavy rains and

---

4 "Capricorn." Living Hope, n.d. http://www.livinghope.co.za/about/communities/capricorn/.

freezing temperatures in the South African winter and fires during the hot and dry summers. These homes also do not provide refuge or safety from theft, active gangs, and widespread drug issues, which result in high crime and violence rates.

Capricorn also sees high rates of domestic violence and abuse, high rates of alcoholism, and prostitution, which leads to a high number of street children. An estimated 20 percent of residents are HIV+, while many more have likely been exposed. There is no medical clinic in the township or the immediate area.[5]

---

5   ISSAfrica.org. "Is Mob Violence out of Control in South Africa?" ISS Africa, March 5, 2019. https://issafrica.org/iss-today/is-mob-violence-out-of-control-in-south-africa.

"It is not our differences that divide us. It is our inability to recognize, accept, and celebrate those differences."

—AUDRE LORDE

DONAVAN AND PAOLA

The Guatemalan Civil War, which lasted from 1960 to 1996, was the longest civil war in Latin America's history. Rooted in five hundred years of violence and exclusion, the working class rebelled against government oppression. During the genocide, over two hundred thousand Guatemalans were killed, of which forty thousand "disappeared." Additionally, many hundreds of thousands of Guatemalans were forcibly displaced.[6]

* * *

Paola: Why we came to the US? Yeah, oh boy. That's a loaded question. All right. Well, Donny and I really didn't have a choice. To be completely honest, I thought we were going

---

6   "Guatemala: The Silent Holocaust." CJA. Center for Justice and Accountability, n.d. https://cja.org/where-we-work/guatemala/.

on a trip, a vacation of sorts. We'd never been on one before, so I really had no idea what to expect. I figured out it wasn't just a trip when we never really returned home. We were young though, ten years old, so to me, it was fun. Life was different. Of course, at the time I didn't realize our "vacation" was actually illegal. When we left home, war was starting to break out.

Donavan: What are you talking about? War wasn't starting to break out. It had already broken out. I mean, remember when Ma and Pappa sat down in the old back room— what would it be called now? Maybe a den is what Jonathan would call it. Jonathan is one of my grandkids. He is darn adorable, especially now that he is out of his sassy phases—pretty smart too. But what was I saying? Oh, yeah, the war. It was surely happening when we were leaving.

Paola: Donny, are you sure that war was declared before we left?

Donavan: I don't know if it was officially declared, but doggone it, why does that really even matter? People were getting shot in the street. Little kids could get their hands on drugs. I mean, I know I did.

Paola: And thank the heavens you didn't get picked up to deal.

Donavan: So, yeah, that was war. I didn't and still don't need a government or someone to tell me what war is. That was it. I saw it with my own eyes. That was war.

Paola: Too many people lost far too much when we were there, and I can't imagine how many more lost, lost, just everything after we left.

Donavan: Remember that boy you had been with? Oh, what was his name? I know it. It's just not coming to me right now.

Paola: Who?

Donavan: Oh, like there were so many. The one who got picked up for dealing. Oh, what's his name? I know it, umm.

Paola: Oh. Jim, from three doors down.

Donavan: Yeah, Jim. I never told you this then. We would ride in the back of his brother-in-law's pickup at night and try to catch deals in action.

Paola: For heaven's sake, why would you do that?

Donavan: It was a game. Quite plainly stupid, now that I think of it. But at the time it was fun, until it started getting too real. We would go around trying to see how much security there was and where we could jump the fences. We would always dare each other to do it, but none of us ever had the guts to go through with it. Now that I'm thinking about it, living in Guatemala was a different experience altogether.

Paolo: I don't think "different" does the experience justice. It was both wonderful and quite terrible at the same time. At the time, it was all we ever knew. But now, I barely even remember living there.

Donavan: How do you not remember? I guess you were a couple years younger than me. But I mean, even now, after being in the United States for so long—it's been almost fifty years, I believe—to me, home is still the one-bedroom shack house we all lived in. You really don't remember it at all?

Paola: I remember bits and pieces. Like I remember how in the evenings, we would sit on the floor of the kitchen and watch the evening news on the pixelated TV set while Ma and Pappa would sit on the two chairs at the table and talk, half-listening to the news report. I remember the plates that we ate from so clearly. Both of our plates were compartmentalized, with three sections on the top and one large section in the center, the size of a piece of bread. Mine had pictures of Winnie the Pooh and yours had pictures of Batman.

Donavan: It was actually Superman.

Paola: Same difference. Ma would put rice in one of the top compartments, beans in another, bread in the center, and a different surprise in the last spot. I loved when it was green grapes or dates. I wasn't a huge fan of figs, but I wasn't really that picky either.

Donavan: It's not like we had much of a choice to be picky. It was either eat what Ma put on the plate, or stay hungry. I loved when the surprise was sliced apples, especially red apples. Those were always just so hard to find. Ma and Pappa really did do their best with us and for us. On my birthday, every year, Pappa would bring home a bar of chocolate, a bag of pretzels, and two apples. All my favorite things. Looking back now, I can't imagine how expensive the chocolate and pretzels must have been, especially closer to the 1960s, when the war conditions started getting bad.

Paola: Pappa had a knack for somehow always making sure he brought us our favorite things on our birthdays. For my birthday, Pappa would bring me a small handcrafted finger doll from the market. They were about the size of my pinky and were made from twine and fabric. When we came to America, I think I had around seven or eight of them in my possession. Ma would tell me how when she was little, she always wanted small finger puppets for her birthday, but that her family couldn't afford them, so she never got them. So when Pappa proposed to Ma, he did it by putting a small ring in a finger puppet. But even if he hadn't proposed in a cute way, Ma still would've said yes.

Donavan: You see, it wasn't about the marriage proposal, or even about the would-be union between the two of them. It was more about the family. And not so much about the marriage between Ma and Pappa combining the two families, even. It was a way to ensure that Ma, who came from a family that was much poorer and really struggled to make ends meet, would be in a better situation. And that her future kids, us, would be able to have access to more opportunities than she did when growing up.

Paola: Ma was the middle child of nine brothers. She was the only daughter in the family, so getting her married off was a very big deal. It was insurance in a way. She also got married very young, at around twelve years of age. That wouldn't happen today. Her wedding wasn't big and glamorous, like they are today. It was more of a formality. They signed the papers in court, and then Ma moved in with Pappa, and they started their life together. They didn't know each other before they got married. It was an arranged marriage, but that was pretty normal at the time.

Donavan: But Pau, it still happens now too. One of our cousins, Gualdiña, just got married, actually. It was also an arranged marriage.

Paola: It was, but it was different. I mean, she knew the fella. It was just that the parents started the conversation and put the prospect of holy matrimony on the table. Ma and Pappa didn't know each other at all before they got married. They didn't even know who the other was, and I don't think they'd ever even seen each other in passing. Kind of a crazy concept to me.

Donavan: Even though Ma got married when she was really just a child, she didn't have me until she was twenty, and the Paola three years later. Ma had a miscarriage before me, though. Really late into the term too, I think. That was when she was eighteen. She was pretty devastated and took it really hard. So they didn't try again for another two years.

Paola: It's crazy to think there could have been three of us, instead of just the two of us. But the world works in mysterious ways, and everything truly is meant to happen. I strongly believe that. I don't believe in coincidences. I just believe in the universe. If things are meant to happen, they happen. And if they're not meant to happen, they don't.

Donavan: So anyway, about Ma and Pappa. After they got married and had us, war had broken out or was starting to break out or whatever. At the time, Ma used to work by cleaning other families' houses. She used to work in the nice part of town. I think it's still too fancy for us, even now.

Paola: I remember Pappa and her would hitch a ride to the mill where Pappa worked with Mr. Ramon. From there, Ma would still have to walk and then catch a bus and then walk some more to the house. I went with Ma once because I missed the bus to school and she couldn't drop me off, but I was too young to be at home alone.

Donavan: Ma liked working there. She said that if you kept to yourself, no one bothered you. But that sometimes, people were quite rude because they thought because they had more money, they were better people than you. Which isn't true, obviously.

Paola: Ma and Pappa drilled that into our heads. Telling us that money doesn't make you a good person, it's you that makes you a good person—your relationships with other people and your relationships with yourself.

Donavan: I don't think I would have been able to work with people who thought they were better than me just because they wore fancy clothes and drove cars, but Ma did. She was a different kind of strong. Well, one day while working at one of the fancy ladies' homes, she overheard them talking about how they were leaving. She didn't know to where but figured it was worth trying to look around for another job, just because she didn't want to be left hanging completely out of the blue, which would mean that half the income our family made would be lost.

Paola: That's one thing that was unique about our family. I mean, there were and are a lot of things that are unique about our family. But where we lived, especially back then, Ma making the same amount of money as Pappa wouldn't have been okay in most households. Some families, like the Rickeys a couple doors down, had their missus take a pay cut and start working less hours so that she wasn't making more than the mister.

Donavan: I mean, God forbid that the wife makes more, or even the same as, the husband. In our house, that would've never passed. If Ma was working hard and earning money for it, Pappa sure as heck would have never asked her to work for less or anything like that.

Paola: I think it's the small things like that, that we all picked up on. The Rickeys' daughter, Claire, still doesn't believe that it's right for a woman to work if she's got a baby at home. I mean, I understand wanting to stay at home and taking care of your child, there's nothing wrong with that. But she, at her core, doesn't believe that she is allowed to work some days and that her man can stay home and take care of the child other days.

Donavan: So when Ma told me this story, she told it to me like this. She said that the missus in charge called her into the parlor. Ma thought she was getting fired because the missus was going to tell her they were moving out of the city. Well, part of that was true, and part of it wasn't. She did call Ma in to tell her they were moving. But they weren't just moving out of the city; they were moving out of the whole country. Her brother had been able to secure her, her husband, and their small one-month-old baby visas to go to America.

Paola: Her brother had all sorts of connections, so it wasn't surprising at all.

Donavan: She told Ma that because of all the unrest, they thought it would be best for them to get out altogether and to start a new life, hopefully a better one.

Paola: Which is a lot to say, considering I didn't think their life was that bad. I mean, living in this big house with fancy cars and even having help to clean their clothes and cook their food. But I digress.

Donavan: She told Ma that she should consider leaving for America with her family too. Ma told her that we didn't have connections like them, so we wouldn't be able to get sponsorships or visas or anything like that. But she put the idea in Ma's head and so when she got home, she told Pappa about it.

Paola: This happened around the same time that my school was shut because it wasn't really that safe anymore. I went to the Montessori, and it was outdoors. You just couldn't have that many kids exposed anymore. It was too much liability for the few adults there.

Donavan: I don't know how long Ma and Pappa talked about the idea or who convinced who, if that was even the case. But about three days later, Pappa told me that we were going to maybe move. I remember asking him where, and he never really gave me an answer. He said it would be a nice change of pace.

Paola: Pappa told me that we were going on a trip and to pack all the things that were my favorite so I could keep them with me. We were each allowed to bring a small knapsack with us.

Donavan: I ended up carrying mine and Pau's. Ma and Pappa both had two too. One of Ma's just had some packed food and snacks. I'll never forget the day we left. We left really early in the morning. I'm not sure what time. But it was before the sun came out, and it was pitch black. Maybe 3:00 or 4:00 a.m.? We walked a couple kilometers to the bus stop and waited for what felt like hours but was probably really only thirty or forty minutes. The bus took us to the train station. The stop we were supposed to get off on was about eight towns over. If we were to have gone by car, it would have taken maybe nine or ten hours. But because the train stops very frequently, every couple kilometers, it took us about twenty-two hours. I remember the train being fine and exciting for the first couple hours, and then the brighter it got outside, the more people came on, the more crowded it became, the hotter it felt, and the more crankier we got.

Paola: I wasn't a big fan of the train. It was quite rickety and made my stomach hurt. I remember feeling nauseous for the majority of those long hours.

Donavan: From the train, Pappa's friend's uncle picked us up from the station. We stayed at their home for a couple hours during the day to get cleaned up and rest for a bit. We left their house and started walking to the next town over when it got dark that night. I think it would have been much easier and faster to take the train. But it also would have been much more expensive.

Paola: I remember walking a good bit, but I also remember Pappa carrying me on his back. The road was hot under our shoes, even when the sun wasn't out.

Donavan: When we got to the town, we went to someone else's house. I'm not entirely sure how we knew them, but they had agreed to let us borrow their car in exchange for some money.

Paola: That was the first time I'd ever seen Pappa drive a car. I wasn't even sure he knew how to. It was also the first time that the four of us had been the only ones in a car.

Donavan: When we were settling into the car, I remember Pappa was writing down a lot of things. I found out on the drive that it was specific instructions on how and where to leave the car when we were done with it. After us, a different family who was trying to get back into the country would take it, and it would eventually find its way home.

I didn't know this at the time, but apparently the car rightfully belonged to the friend who we borrowed it from because he had paid for it. But the person that he had bought it from had stolen the car, so the plates were actually mock-ups. It's a good thing that we never got pulled over or anything because we would have had to pay a large fine that we definitely would not have been able to afford.

Paola: Maybe that's why we drove through the night.

Donavan: I think we did that because there were less cars on the road and Pappa had never really driven before. I don't really remember exactly what happened after that and where we went from place to place. Do you, Pau?

Paola: I remember even less than you. I remember when we finally reached the US border fence, Ma was in tears.

Donavan: I guess before we got to the checkpoint, I remember walking a lot. We walked for weeks, I am sure of it. Every evening or so, we would sleep on our knapsacks, taking turns staying up. Even when it was Pappa's turn to sleep, he would always stay up and say that he was just keeping either Ma or I company. But I'm sure it was because he felt that if anything happened on his watch, he would be responsible.

Paola: Even in the middle of nowhere, Ma and Pappa would still take the time to sing a lullaby so that I could drift off to sleep. It's those little things that always remind me of how much they loved us and how much they truly did everything for us.

Donavan: Ma packed a good amount of food in the knapsack, but after a couple of days, we were running low. When we were driving, Pappa would pull over at small gas stations to pick up some more food and water. But when we were walking, we didn't really come across any of those places, so we had to start rationing. It was good that Pau was young and didn't really have that big of an appetite anyway. This sounds pretty bad, but it was good in a way if one of us wasn't feeling well and couldn't really eat. It wasn't good, but it was good for the food supply. After days of walking, I remember Pappa saying, "I think we're here." I was really confused.

Paola: If you were confused, imagine how confused I was. I thought we were going on a trip and from where we were standing, it definitely didn't seem to be the dream vacation Ma had told me about. At least you knew that we were moving.

Donavan: In the journey and at night when we were sleeping, Pappa told me that we were going to America. I didn't believe him at first. I didn't know much about it, but from what I did know, only smart and rich people lived there. Why were we going to go? We wouldn't fit in. I also thought he was joking because I did know that it was far and that even if you got there, they didn't have these magic open gates to let anyone in. I asked why we were even trying if we could get sent away. Pappa said that if we didn't try, there was no chance we were going to maybe have the opportunity to live a better life in the United States. But, if we did try, just maybe, our life could change for the best. But when Pappa said that we had arrived, I remember actually thinking that he must be joking. There was no sign that said "Welcome to the United States," no American flags, nothing showing us that we were in a completely different country with a supposed completely different quality-of-life standard.

Paola: Well, that was kind of the point, though. If we had seen "Welcome to the United States" banners, that would have been a dead giveaway that we were definitely in the wrong location.

Donavan: I know, but it just wasn't like I imagined, I suppose. One thing that did change was how serious Ma and Pappa got. I remember at one time Pau was whining, and they both got extremely scared that someone would hear us or notice us. I caught on and didn't say a word until Pappa explicitly said I could. When we got close to the lake, it wasn't hard to stay quiet. It was much louder than all of us. The rushing of the water drowned out my own thoughts, much less any sound coming from the area.

Paola: Donny, it wasn't a lake. It was a river. The Rio Grande.

Donavan: The goal was to spend the night in a friend of Ma's boss's home. But as we got closer into the city, the dark sky was lightening. Pappa made an executive decision, and we didn't go to their home. We went to a church instead. The feeling of entering that church was one that I wish I could relive every day of my life. When we entered through the church and could see the sanctuary, a wave of relief washed over me. Ma sank to the ground, weeping. Pappa knelt down beside her, holding her close as silent tears ran down his cheeks too. We were safe.

Paola: We spent a little more than a week in the haven of that church, helping cook and clean to earn our stay as well.

Donavan: From there, we went from house to house, once even the back barn of a rancher. I'm still shocked by all the families that took us into their homes, knowing that we were putting them at risk. When Ma and Pappa passed, three and a half months apart from each other, neither of them were citizens. It made it difficult to give them a proper funeral ceremony, but their sacrifices are what made our life possible today.

Paola: I think they're resting peacefully now. Yeah. I think they are.

Donavan: We're citizens now, yeah. I married Santiago and Donny married Lydia, who were both citizens.

Paola: We didn't marry for citizenship, though.

Donavan: No, no, we didn't. We married for love.

> *"Let the beauty of what you love be what you do."*
> —RUMI

KABIRA

I walk the streets of Karachi, feeling the potholes of the uneven footpath beneath my feet. The nauseatingly sweet smell of fresh ladoo reminds me that I haven't eaten a proper meal since leaving the United States. I pass a pani-puri stall and consider stopping for a quick snack. I haven't had the small crispy bowls of chickpeas, diced onions, and tangy chutney in over nine years, not since the last time I came back to Pakistan.

"Kabira! Kabira! Aap vapis ghar agaye?"

I look around. It is Ahmed Uncle, two stalls down, selling churiya bangles. I am not home, I explain, but just visiting. And no, I am still, in fact, not married. I bid him farewell, telling him my dadi and dada must be wondering where I am. I dropped my suitcases off at their apartment earlier this morning, insisting they go to the bazaar to get groceries for the week without me. The knot in my stomach keeps me from giving in and ordering a bowl of fresh sabazi.

I can't help but letting my mind wander to the reason I am here. My grandparents are such an important part of who I am. Every June for the past decade of my life, I remember running out of the customs gate searching the arrivals area for the balding head of my dada and the colorful shawls of my dadi. But how they will react to my change in plans?

It will be dark soon. I hurry along the path towards my grandparents' home, getting honked at by a rickshaw. How is it possible that the last time I came to Karachi I was in middle school? I spent every summer until I was thirteen in these streets with my cousins, arguing over what Bollywood movie we would watch and which candy stalls we would visit that day.

Dadi would call the girls from outside before lunch and force us into helping her prepare the meals for that day. I would beg her to let me keep playing football with the boys, but she would wipe the dirt from my forehead, help me put my shoes back on, brush the leaves out of my hair, and simply say, "*Nei, aap to lurki he.*" I would cross my arms and say it wasn't fair that I was a girl. I didn't choose to be one. So, why couldn't I keep playing?

And before I knew it, I would be crying in the airport, begging my parents to let me stay for even a week longer. But the summer was over, and so it was time to go back to the States for school. In America there were no kids playing on the streets, carefree and without shoes. There were no stalls along the roadside selling snacks and desserts. There were no cars honking excessively at each other. There was no dadi and no dada.

I enter through the compound's gate and nod hello to the lala who is keeping watch for the night. I open the iron gate with a number five above it and climb the four flights of stairs to my grandparents' flat. A little out of breath, I knock on the door, waiting for my dada to open it. A yellow light turns on at the end of the hallway, and I can hear the creaking of his walker and his light footsteps down the hallway. He opens the door for me and immediately takes me in his arms. His musky cologne envelops me.

The house is exactly as I remember it. Immediately next to the door is the wooden dining table where I spent so many meals excitedly telling my grandparents about how my day had gone. Just beyond it is the kitchen, where I would stand on a stool and practice making perfectly round chapatis with my dadi. To its side is the study, where my dada would teach me practical skills every week, like how to balance a checkbook or how to optimize grocery trips for efficiency, shopping with detailed lists. And my dada. I haven't seen him in years, but his arms feel like home. I have missed his gentle light gray eyes, his comforting voice, and his fondness for sweater vests. He is a soft man with strong feelings.

"*Kabira, ghar pe agiye?*"

Emerging from the kitchen is my dadi, with an apron tied around her waist and flour dusted on her cheeks. She takes off her oven mitts and rests them on the wooden dining table. She kisses me on my forehead and scans my body to see how I am faring since the last time she saw me, which was this morning. She immediately takes me by my elbows and ushers me to sit down to eat. I ask her if she needs help.

"Do you want *madat*?"

She brings plate after plate of food and sets them down in the center of the table: a bowl of nihari, a plate of biryani, small dishes of raita and cachumber, and a platter of fresh naan. My dada takes a seat at the head of the table, and my dadi immediately starts to fill his plate and then mine. When our plates are overflowing with food, she runs to the kitchen for glasses of water and cutlery. After setting them down, she insists that the nihari must be getting too cold and offers to warm it up.

"*Neigh, niegh. Aap aabi khali bhet.*" My dada insists that she sit and eat with us. That is typical of my dadi: ensuring that there is an abundance of fresh, warm, food on the table and refusing to eat until everyone else has. I tear a piece of naan off and dip it into my portion of nihari. I think what I missed most about Karachi, besides my grandparents, of course, was the food.

"*To beta, aap vapis Pakistan aare he?*" But I don't think I could ever move back. I'm too American for Pakistan, and not American enough for Texas. My English has a foreign accent, and my Urdu has an American one. Moving back to Karachi would only confuse me more.

"*Neigh dada*, I can't move back yet. My life is in America now." We talk about how my flight was. We talk about their day at the market. We talk about my little sisters and how they are doing. We talk about my parents and how they are doing. We talk about the political state of the US and Pakistan. And then we talk about me.

"Dada, Dadi. While studying and travelling this past year, I have found myself exploring who I am. Through art." I nervously fiddle with the two rings on my finger before forcing myself to cross my hands and leave them settled in my lap.

"*Shabash, beta.* That is very good." Dadi smiles at me, encouraging me to go on.

"And I have found that I want to pursue it. It is my passion, and I really enjoy painting."

"But med school *ko kya hoyga*?" Dada asks. He takes a sip of water, waiting for me to respond.

"My art feels more important to me than going back to school right now." I push the sweat-stuck pieces of hair off the back of my neck and tie them into a loose ponytail at the nape of my neck.

"Medicine is an art too." He smiles.

I don't laugh.

"*Nahi beta*. You cannot do this. *Hamari* family *me* doctors and engineers *hai*. We are not a family of artists. We are professionals." He gently folds the napkin on his lap into a neat square before forcefully setting it down beside his plate.

"But Dada, I am not interested in those fields as much as I am in my paintings. Those fields are not my passion." I look at my dadi, but she stays silent.

"*Humlog badme baath kharenge. Aap abhi sau ja aur rest khar,*" my dada says, saving the conversation for another time as he stands from the table and goes to rest in his room.

My dadi stands to clear the dishes, gently stacking the dirty plates on top of each other. She sets them in the sink and returns to the kitchen table for the remaining bowls. I watch her spoon the leftover nihari into a plastic Tupperware box with such care. She does the same for the biryani. She gently sets the empty dishes down in the sink and pours green dish washing liquid onto a sponge. I walk to the counter and wrap the remaining pieces of naan in a piece of tin foil and carry it along with the Tupperware containers to a shelf in the fridge.

My dadi washes each of the dirty dishes, using as much care as she did when brushing the tangles out of my hair. I join her beside the sink and grab the hand towel off the counter. She passes a white glass plate with a navy-blue trim of flowers to me. I shake the excess water off of it and dry it with my towel, laying it down in the rack gently after I finish. She continues to pass me dishes, and I continue to work until there are no more dirty dishes. I pass her the hand towel, and she wipes her hands. "*Beta, aap kho artist khuy banahe.*"

Why do I want to be an artist? Each time I stand in front of my easel, opening the wooden drawer to unveil an array of different brushes and tubes, I am at ease. I pick a single tube and feel the cold metal cap press against my fingers as I twist it off, careful not to exert too much pressure, which would result in dripping paint. I run my fingers along the heads of my collection of paintbrushes, feeling the difference between the rough and the soft, the long and the short, the small and the large bristles.

Sitting on the edge of my stool with a blank canvas in front of me, I am in control. I have the power to take this blank piece of fabric stapled to a wooden frame and make it mine. To make it something that people want to see. To make it something that my family is proud of. To make it something that I am proud of. But how can I explain all of this to my dadi and dada?

I shake my head, not having a proper answer to my grandmother's question for her yet. I hug her goodnight, comforted by the lavender scent of her hair and the feel of her shalwar kameez against me. I settle into the room that belonged to my father when he was growing up. I open my suitcase and unpack my essentials for the night, removing the two pairs of shoes I brought with me and setting them down on the floor beside the mattress.

I gently pad down the hallway to the one bathroom in the apartment and softly close the door behind me, setting my toiletries beside the sink. The bathroom is small but has all the essentials. Immediately to the left of the sink is a shower curtain shielding a rusty shower head and faucet, a shelf of shampoos, and a squat hole in the ground that acts as both a toilet and a drain for the shower. I turn the water knob to warm to wash my face but am instead left with a lukewarm drip. I run my fingers under the sporadic flow of water before splashing it onto my face. I rub the worn-down hand towel against my face and grab my belongings before heading back to my room.

I settle into bed and pull the blankets around me. Resting my head on my pillow, I run my fingers along the frayed edges of the comforter in search of sleep. I hear a light knock on the door before my dada peeks his head in wishing me a good night. "Sorry for being so harsh earlier today, beta. I only want what is best for you, my *jaanemun*."

"I know, Dada."

"*Gudafez, beta.*"

"Goodnight, Dada."

* * *

A small sliver of sunlight finds its way through the gap of the blinds. I glance at the bedside alarm clock. It isn't even seven yet. The sweet smell of chola puri pulls me out of my half-asleep daze. I sit at the edge of the mattress and attempt to pat down the frizz of my hair. I slip on a pair of socks before standing up to open the blinds fully, letting myself be blinded by the morning Karachi sun for a second before turning as I hear my dadi call out my name.

I make my way to the kitchen. It looks much worse in the daylight than it did last night. There is rusty gas stove crammed in the corner by the window, which would most definitely be a hazard if there were still young children in the home. Beside the stove is a clay tandoor to make fresh naan, with a hot water heater stacked on top of it. Yet another fire hazard. To the immediate left of the entry way of the kitchen is the sink and drying rack that has the dishes I helped clean from last night. The kitchen is so tiny, yet I still cannot seem to locate my dadi.

I hear her small voice from behind me, and she emerges from the hallway closet, four different spice containers in hand. My dadi's wooden spice rack, which has found its home on three walls of the coat closet, is more than it seems. It serves as a testament to the ability of unique flavors that can be created from a combination of mere pigments. The distinct flavor of cardamom and the fiery reds of saffron transport me into the thirteenth century, a time of Islamic emperors and regal moguls. She uses her spices as a medium through which to channel her passion. She gives the spices power, the same power I hope my art will have on others.

"*Beta, abhi khana khane aaja,*" she says, ushering me to the table and setting down three different dishes, two short pitchers of milk and aam ka raas, and a glass of water. She says that my dada has gone down the street to pick up a prescription for the medicine he needs for his deteriorating eyes but will be returning before it is time to take the offerings to the Jamatkhana, our place of prayer.

"Kabira…," she trails on, but I am mesmerized by the way she says my name. It sounds like velvet as it flows from her mouth. When I was younger, I used to despise my name. I couldn't find it on the travel keychains or touristy T-shirts that lined the walls of the overpriced amusement park gift shops. I would scan the rotating shelves, desperate to find my name on a little license plate or in between the silvery specks of a snow globe but would always turn away in dismay. My name was never there.

But Kabira has grown on me. Each letter is laced with history, whether from this era or another. As lavish kings and queens indulge in ethnic delicacies served on fine china and sit around on handwoven Oriental rugs, they sip their piping hot tea and discuss the land of Kabira: the land of opportunity, the land of the greatest and the most powerful. My name flashes me back to a time when hundreds of Arabian scholars were gathered in dingy libraries as they manually copied calligraphy on to papyrus scrolls. As they worked late into the night, they dipped their feather pens into small pots of ink and longed for a Kabiruna when the sun rose, or a wondrous morning in old script Arabic. My Arabian name evokes thoughts of my ancient ancestors and their daily lives: how they brushed their teeth, washed their clothes, cooked their rice, and made the most beautiful triptychs littered with geometric shapes, arabesques, and unique ceramics.

"*Kabira jaan?*"

"Sorry, Dadi, what were you saying?"

"Beta, your dada and I just want you to be happy. Your happiness means much more to us than two letters before your name and a lab coat ever could."

Wiping my hands on a rumal, I look up to her. "I know, Dadi. I just don't want to disappoint either of you."

She stands up and wraps me in her embrace, the sweet smell of the honey from this morning's breakfast lingering on her sari. "You could never disappoint us, Kabira."

As my dadi picks up the bowls and plates from the table, neatly stacking them as she goes, the rusted door creaks open. With several khapre bags, my dada walks in. My dadi pops her head out of the kitchen alcove and greets him. I relieve him of the bags and unload them on the table. Glancing through the bags, I can see the loot he has: fresh beets, arugula, and an assortment of other fruits and vegetables for my dadi in a couple bags, a container of borderline too-sweet peshwari ice cream, and his eye medication in another bag.

He wraps me in an embrace. Each time he hugs me, it feels like the first hug from him in years: warm, tight, and with very little sign of who will be the first one to let go. I stay wrapped in his arms a little longer each time because I am not sure which hug may be the last.

* * *

The flight attendants make their way through the aisle, working to ensure all tray tables are stowed and all seat backs are in their upright position. The wheels of the Boeing 707 touch the tarmac, and I can feel the warm Texas sun radiating its blistering heat through the shaded windows. The pilot switches off the seatbelt sign and all 200 passengers simultaneously stand. The wailing of babies is replaced by the opening and closing of bags and bins.

While waiting for the cabin doors to open, I switch my phone back on and am flooded by an influx of text messages from my mother asking for my ETA and WhatsApp messages from my dadi and dada. I grab my duffel bag from the overhead bin, carefully trying not to let it fall, or worse, hit someone, in the process. After thanking the air hostesses on my way out of the aircraft, I make my way to the immigration line.

The floor to ceiling windows of the George Bush Intercontinental Airport flood the area with light. I shrug out of my designated plane jacket and tie it around my waist. A line of soon-to-be flyers are already lined up, waiting to board the plane I just got out of. There is an infant crawling around on the floor, swerving her way through small suitcases, and a frantic young dad trying to keep up while calling out her name in desperation. There is a wheelchair-bound man waiting in the preboarding area with a TSA agent gently waiting by his side. There is a teen engrossed in his Nintendo game console with black headphones covering his ears. There is what seems to be a newly married couple giddily waiting to board.

The buzzing of my phone snaps me out of my people watching daze. I pick up and hear my mother frantically asking if I have made it through immigration yet. "No, no. I'm heading there now," I say, promising to call her as soon as I get through the last checkpoint and claim my luggage.

As I make my way to the final checkpoint, I notice the awfully long lines outside the women's restroom and, contrarily, what seems to be an easy flow of in-and-out for the men's room. After every hundred steps, there is a bakery or a restaurant selling carbohydrate-loaded dishes to antsy travelers. Almost each eatery is matched with at least one, if not two, gift shops selling "Don't Mess with Texas" merchandise on anything and everything, from sweatshirts to pencil pouches.

After waiting a seemingly long fifteen minutes, I step up to the immigration officer's booth. I leaf through my handbag, reaching for my passport. He opens the blue cover up to the worn-down page with an outdated picture of me.

"Kabira Kajani?"

"Yes, sir."

"How long were you in Pakistan?"

"Four days, sir."

"And what were you doing there?"

"Visiting my grandparents, sir."

He instructs me to look into the small camera attached to the back of his computer screen. I remove my glasses and wait for the red light to blink. "Welcome home, Miss Kajani," he says, stamping my passport and returning it to me. I grab my handbag and duffel and make my way to the other side of the gate, taking a moment to get my things together. I open my handbag and put my passport back in its designated spot. A small, worn, brown leather sketchbook catches my attention. I look around to see who it could belong to. It is in my bag, but it definitely isn't mine. I have never seen it before.

I take the small book in my hands and open the cover, hoping to find the name of its owner written inside. With no luck, I leaf through the pages. Each page is empty. Before closing the book, I catch a small inscription on the inside of the back cover. I try my best to translate the writing to English. A tear falls down my cheek as I read my dada's scrawny handwriting.

> *This world is yours, Kabira.*
> *With our love and blessings,*
> *Your dadi and dada*

"To exist is to survive unfair choices"

—THE OA

PABLITO
PART 2

January 25th

Pa came home today. The last time he came home was in November, and that was only for two days. This time, he was able to get leave for four. Ma was able to get off work in the afternoon today, so we went to a taqueria for lunch. It was really nice. All of us haven't sat down at the table and eaten together in so long. Penelope is getting older too, so there was a lot more talking than there has ever been before. And I have to admit, it was so much fun.

We also ate so much food. I can't even remember, but we had chips and salsa, lots of cheese quesadillas (Cara's favorite), frijoles, enchiladas, and rice. We even went to a raspa place after for snow cones. I got one with half tiger's blood and half blue coconut. I was going to get cream on top, but it was a dollar extra and I felt bad for spending so much, so I didn't.

After lunch, Ma had to go back to the office building she cleans for the evening janitorial shift. Everyone was so tired that we just went back home to rest. Cara was out like a light even on the car ride back home. It didn't take long before Penelope and Sebastian were asleep too. I helped Pa carry them into the house and took a nap myself too.

For dinner, Pa made arroz con pollo. It was so good. I told him he would have to leave me the recipe, but he laughed and said his was nothing in comparison to Ma's. I miss Ma's cooking. Before she had the night job, she would cook for us and put it in the refrigerator so we could heat it up and eat it the next day.

But circumstances have changed since, so I've gotten used to heating up the frozen packets for us. I've actually gotten pretty good at making the serving sizes stretch too. Boxes that are marked to be for a meal, I can make last for three meals for all four of us by adding a small side of rice or cutting up some carrots to go with it.

I also decided that I would table the college talk for tomorrow.

January 27th

Yesterday, we went to the beach. I hadn't been in so long, and it was so much fun. Much better than I remember it. Of course, we had to be very careful because the waves were kind of big and Penelope and Cara are so young. Both of them were wearing the arm floaties, and it was so adorable. Sebastian and I spent some time on a wakeboard. I went under more than just a couple of times, but it was still one of the best days I've had in a while.

I think that's also because it was nice to have someone else around who was responsible. It was nice to have Pa around. I didn't have to worry about Cara and Penelope and Sebastian; I just had to worry about me. It sounds selfish, but it really was nice to not have to think about anyone, or everyone, else.

After playing in the water for a bit, we all retracted (SAT word!) back to the sand. We covered Sebastian in sand while he was laying down and then decided to pool our resources together to make the most epic sandcastle to ever exist. Penelope would run back and forth from the sand to the water to collect buckets of water for the moat we built around our castle. Sebastian and I worked diligently (another SAT word, heck yeah) to not only achieve great volume of each of the towers but also height. Pa's main role was to keep Cara occupied so that she wouldn't unknowingly bring our structure to a premature demise. I think we had a total of nine castle towers, a full moat, and a small flag flying overhead before it started to crumble. Cara ran in as it was and jumped on it, making it crumble even quicker.

While I cleaned off the buckets in the water, Pa dried everyone off and flagged down the ice cream truck for a sweet treat. He handed me a chocolate dipped drumstick: my favorite. I didn't think Pa would remember, but I was a mix of genuinely surprised and ecstatic that he did. Licking off all the chocolate first, I watched as Cara nibbled with her one tooth at the end of a rainbow popsicle, how the juice of the lemon slush dripped down Penelope's chin, and how Sebastian was intensely concentrating on his ice cream sandwich. I can't explain it as well as I wish I could, but just looking at them, I felt so incredibly happy and content to be where I was. I mean, these humans are some of the weirdest ones out there, but they're mine.

Also, decided to table to the college convo one more day.

January 28th

Pa left around noon today. I woke up extra early to make sure that I could talk to him and Ma together before Ma had to go to work. I wrote out my talking points last night, which was really just a concise summary of all the papers the counselors have been giving us at school. Like, I wrote down important things about the SAT, like the cost, but left out the date and time and stuff.

Well, anyway. It went a lot better than I thought. I also made eggs and coffee in the morning to butter Ma and Pa up before the conversation. There were four pieces of bacon hidden in the freezer, so I even fried those. There was actually a fifth one, but there was some white goo on it, which I think was mold, so I made the executive decision to toss that piece out. We can't afford another sick one in this household, literally.

Ma and Pa were surprised when they came to the kitchen to already see me there, but I think, deep down, they also knew that this conversation would have to happen eventually.

I'll spare you all the details, but I will say there was a lot of tearing up (Ma), some yelling (Pa…and me), and a lot of hugging (all three of us). Ma started to tear up when I said that I wanted to go to college and get a four year education instead of just an associate's degree. She said that us having that option and us thinking about doing things like getting a higher education is the reason that she and Pa moved to the United States. Pa was just as excited but was a little more worried about the logistics (mostly the financial stuff) of it.

Applying to a university in itself is very costly on its own. It is not just the price of the SAT tests, but it also costs money to send my transcript and a good $80–$100 for just the application fee itself. I showed both of them the papers the counselor had given me, explaining how there are fee waivers for people whose family makes less than a certain level of income each year. We definitely qualify, so I assured them that the application portion of the process wouldn't cost us any money.

But I couldn't say the same thing about actually going to college. That is, if I even get accepted anywhere. I told Ma and Pa that I would apply for scholarships and loans, and take them out in my name and everything, so hopefully that will cover the cost. I mean, it has to. Ma and Pa won't really be able to help me out financially. I would be stupid if I thought otherwise.

In summary (my English teacher doesn't really like when I use this phrase in my essays, but I think it makes me sound professional), Ma and Pa said I can take the SAT and apply to a college, but that I should probably only apply to schools in the state because out of state gets expensive (in terms of actually getting there and living and stuff, which I hadn't really even considered, but that's a valid point).

I asked what would happen to the kids, who would take them to school and everything. Ma said that that should be the last of my worries and that they will figure it out and everything will be okay. That was really reassuring. I don't want Sebastian to have to quit soccer because he doesn't have anyone to take him to practice, and Penelope was getting excited about the idea of maybe starting ballet classes. It was nice to hear Ma and Pa both say that education should be my first priority and that they will always be there for me.

Our family isn't the most perfect, for sure. And when I say that (or write, I guess), I mean, we aren't the most typical. We don't have family dinners together every night. Ma doesn't pack our lunches or volunteer to help at the science fair. Pa doesn't participate in safety patrol in the mornings to help kids out of the car. But I do think that the kids and I are closer than most siblings are. We're all we have. I like knowing that I can count on my family and that they can count on me. Something inside tells me that good things are on the horizon.

January 29th

I GOT THE JOB!!!!! I got a call this morning from Christi, who is the manager, saying that I got the job. Carl found out yesterday that he got the job too! I start working on February 1st. Christi told me to come in as soon as possible to pick up my uniform and to set my hours. So, Carl and I went. My uniform is really just a name tag and the red company

T-shirt. Technically, we are supposed to wear khaki pants too, but because we work so early in the morning, when there aren't too many customers there, she said we are allowed to wear jeans.

Carl decided that he wanted to work Monday–Friday from 2:00–6:00 a.m. I chose the same times and days because they worked perfectly for me and because I didn't really have transportation to get to work other than Carl. I'm so happy we're going to be working together. He's a really great friend and always offers to drive me anywhere. Once I get my first paycheck, I think I'll give a small portion of it to him to cover the gas costs. We live close, but it's really not thaaat close.

Christi said that we start at minimum wage, but every six months, we get an automatic $0.50 pay raise (as long as we aren't bad employees). That means by the end of senior year, I could be making $170 every week. I can't even explain how much that will help around the house. Plus my soccer gig!!

Ma and Pa told me to put half of my paycheck into saving every week to get started on the savings for college. I think that's a great idea, so I'm going to try to do that. I also have to go open my own bank account so that my paycheck can be deposited there. There is too much adulting happening right now, but I'm excited.

January 30th

I went to the bank today, and turns out I'm not old enough to open my own account. It gets worse. Ma and Pa are hesitant to cosign on the account with me because they don't have papers and don't want to take that risk, which makes complete sense. So I did some research, and I can still get an account and work and everything if I am financially independent. I talked to my counselor about this, and she said that this would also help in applying for scholarships to college because it shows that I am not getting financial help from my parents.

But becoming financially independent isn't easy. I will have to go to the courthouse and explain to a judge why I want to be so, and only if he thinks that I've presented a good case, can I be. I made an appointment for next week. I talked to Christi, and she said that I technically shouldn't be allowed to work, but after a lot of my pleading, she said that because of my unique circumstances, it should be okay for me to still start working on the first. Wish me luck, because I think this is going to be a long and tiring process.

February 1st

Today was the best first day of work ever! Carl picked me up at one thirty so that we could get there a little early. The night manager, Jon, showed us the ropes. We spent thirty minutes just going through the grocery store and learning where every section is and where to find certain items. It was a little overwhelming just because there's so many items. Jon said that there are probably even more than fifty thousand items in the grocery store, but that we would get used to it over time without a problem.

After that, Carl went to the stocking section and I was assigned to the unloading section. It was kind of therapeutic. I didn't really have to think. It was just unloading crates of milk for three hours, which doesn't sound like fun, but it really was. I could think about anything and everything or absolutely nothing at all. My back hurts a bit, but I think it's because I was getting sloppy toward the end of my shift. Now I know to keep my posture straight, even if it's a little bit annoying.

Carl and I left around six fifteen, right in time to watch the sun rise on Ocean Drive before we headed home. It was the most beautiful sunrise I have ever seen. The sky was painted with oranges and yellows that I've only seen before in art class. The sky cast this vibrant reflection on the water, and I couldn't believe how beautiful this world is. Once the sun started to rise, it came up very quickly.

I actually just got back. I'm going to shower really quick before waking the kids up and making their lunches. Write to you soon, Journal!!!

February 20th

Helllooo, Journal!! I know it's been a while since I've written to you, but life has just been so crazy and so busy, but really in the best way possible.

I'll give you some quick updates. Sebastian won MVP of the winter season for his soccer team, which is so incredible and he is so deserving. It has really been motivating him to work even harder in school so that Ma will let him practice more in the backyard. Penelope started ballet classes at the local YMCA. I love watching her twirl around the living room in her pink slippers. Ma was able to get some ripped ones from a thrift store and patch them up.

For Penelope's birthday, I want to try to see if I can save up and get her a brand new pair. Cara is as cute (and whiny) as ever. She's still teething, so there's been a lot of crying. It sucks to see her in pain, but other than those times, she is always as cute and smiley as ever.

I've still been working during the week every morning with Carl. On Fridays, Roberto, the head baker, always comes in early to make fresh donuts, so he gives us a couple. We've also made it a little tradition or part of our routine to watch the sunrise on Ocean Drive every morning after work before going home. It's definitely my favorite part of the day. It's such a mystery what it's going to look like.

Whether it's going to be shades of red or purple, overcast and cloudy, or a clear sky, whether we can trace the shape of the sun or the if the sky will gradually just change from dark to light. Every sunrise is so different and unique. It blows my mind how there are billions of different combinations of what each day will look like, starting with how the sun will rise, or maybe even before that. It's also very reassuring. I mean, regardless of what kind of day I have, the sun always rises—how cliché (SAT word!!) of me to say.

Anyways, back to my updates!! I'm now legally financially dependent, I got my first paycheck (taxes suck), and I got my first 100 on one of my short responses for English. I've been doing a lot of SAT prep and trying to improve my vocabulary, so I'm glad it's been paying off. The prompt was about my favorite pastime, so I wrote about driving down Ocean Drive with Carl. I'm actually really proud of it. I'll copy it in here so that it's here too:

The wind from the sea tangles the short curls of my hair as I sit in the passenger seat of the car. Cruising down Ocean Drive with Carl is easily one of my favorite pastimes. Each of the small white pagodas lining the sea wall holds a unique special treasure.

Carl slows to a stop at the red light right in front of the famous burger shop founded in this small city by the bay. The drive-thru wraps around the building, and the smell of fries and early morning honey-butter chick biscuits overwhelms me. We continue down the street, cruising past dog walkers and bicycle riders. Carl drives faster in an attempt to make it to the dock right in time for the sunrise. He deftly avoids all the new cones and one-way signs in place and drives down the ramp of the parking lot.

Right where the sky meets the sea, a sliver of yellow peeks out, taunting us, testing whether the day is ready for it yet. The oranges and reds follow, lighting up the sky. Each ray casts a different reflection onto the vast gulf that lays before us. The beauty inspires energy. The birds start to chirp and a few fish jump out of the water because regardless of what happened yesterday, today is a new day.

I think I want to start writing creatively a little more. There's a creative writing scholarship competition that is open to juniors and seniors in May, and I think I might start working on a piece to apply to it. It's a great opportunity. I would get to write for a real purpose and hopefully get some money to add to my scholarship fund too. I've been saving pretty well, which is great, but I'm still nowhere near close to funding my own education. So, that is still very much a work in progress. But everything is going good, write to you tomorrow, Journal!

February 28th

I know I said I would write to you tomorrow, last week, and I never did. So for that, I'm sorry, Journal. To be completely honest, this past week has not been too great. I mean, I knew that this would happen. Everything was going so great for such a long time, I knew that it wouldn't last long. For the first week after things were going good, I prepared myself for the worst. But after that, I let my guard down, and that's my own fault.

My hours at work got cut back a lot. Which means less money and less time with Carl. What's worse is that I think I'm more upset about the latter, which I really shouldn't be. I mean, we're just friends, and it's normal when friends don't see each other every day, I guess.

I was also doing so good saving half of every paycheck, but last Tuesday, a water pipe under the kitchen sink busted. It happened during the day, so the kitchen, the bathroom, and the room that Cara and Penelope sleep in was flooded. Their room doesn't have a proper bed frame because they sleep on an mattress that is tucked into the corner of the room, so their bed was completely ruined too. Sebastian and I tried to fix the pipe, but it was too damaged. Ma had to call a plumber and because they only come during business hours and because they only work in the house if there is at least an eighteen-year old in the house, Ma had to take off work that day. The plumber came and charged an absurd amount for something that took him only thirty minutes to fix. He charged us for not just parts but labor and transportation too.

To make it worse, because there is still so much water in the carpet of the bedroom that we didn't get out fast enough, mold started to grow. Obviously, that's a health hazard, especially for the little ones, so Cara and Penelope have been sleeping on Sebastian and I's bed, and we've been sleeping on blankets on the floor next to them. Pa is coming back the second week of March, so hopefully the mold doesn't spread past their room and he will be able to figure out how to fix it when he's back.

In summary, my rainy-day savings are gone, I'm not making as much as I used to, I don't get to see Carl as much anymore, and there's toxic mold in the house. Oh, and I made an F on my last calculus test. Fan-freaking-tastic.

March 2nd

I went to the Career Center at my high school today. I told the counselor what I was feeling and what Ma and Pa had said, about it being okay to take the SAT and all. I got a fee waiver so that I can take it once without having to pay. Did you know that the SAT costs almost seventy dollars?? Isn't that a bit ridiculous? I'm the one who has to study and sit through such a long test AND I have to pay for it? Ridiculous. I knew that college was going to be expensive, but I didn't realize that even applying for college was sooooo expensive.

My counselor also sat down and made an SAT study plan with me. The library has books with lots of practice exams, so I checked one out. It's one of the thickest books I've ever seen. It's pretty intimidating, I'm not going to lie. But I think with the study plan, it'll be easy to just tackle it in small pieces at a time.

While we were making my study plan, guess who walked into the Career Center too. That's right: Carl. I hadn't seen him in a couple of days. It felt a bit weird and awkward at first. I don't really know why. On my way out of the Career Center, I saw him hanging around the chairs, so I stopped by. I got really excited and weirdly nervous when he told me that he had been waiting for me.

We made plans to take a drive tomorrow after school and grab some coffee and do homework or something. Just kind of hang, you know.

March 3rd

Today was easily the. best. day. ever.

After Calculus, which is my last class of the day, I hung out in the library for forty-five minutes because Carl has one more class after me. I have a free period for the last class period so that I can go pick up the little ones, but Ma said that she could pick them up today so that I could hang out with friends, or just Carl, really.

So, after Carl finished class, we drove to a new burger place that opened up in town. Besides helping pay for the water pipe that burst, I hadn't spent a lot of money. I've actually been really good in trying to save money for college. The burger place was really good, kind of modern looking. It had the tall table, mellow music, hanging light bulbs vibe going on. I ordered a double cheeseburger and fries with a cookies and creme milkshake. I don't even think to say it was the best meal I have ever had would be an understatement.

Carl and I talked about a lot. We talked about school and classes and work and college and summer. We talked about the sibs, both mine and his. We talked about people at school and teachers. We talked about our boss at work. While I remember the burger and fries being really good, I don't really remember eating it. We were talking and eating, and before I knew it, we had both finished our meals, but our conversation hadn't stopped once.

We didn't really know what to do or where to go. The original plan was to just work on homework, but it just didn't seem as fun as doing nothing, so we decided to just drive around town. We listened and made fun of the people calling in to the 6:00 p.m. local radio show as they tried to answer riddles to win concert tickets. We figured out one of the riddles and so I was going to call in, but right before I did, one of the other callers got it right.

We drove to the outskirts of town, where the windmill farms are. I'd seen them in the distance when we were driving, but I had never been so close to them. They were really deserted. So we turned the A/C off to save gas, rolled the windows down, and just drove. They were much bigger than I had imagined, even taller than some buildings. They were a lot louder than I had thought they would be too. So loud that we couldn't hear the music, and so we just turned the radio off for a bit.

I think closer to eight, Carl parked and we just sat on the bed of his truck and watched the sun set. It was fun watching the white blades of the windmills slice the yellows and oranges of the sky. In that moment, I felt not just content, but intensely happy. I could feel it deep in my stomach and my skin. I'm not sure where the feeling was coming from, but I could literally feel in my bones how happy I was. I think it's because in that moment, I realized that I liked Carl. And not just as a friend, but more than that.

I'm not exactly sure what this means. I mean, I do know that I think I'm gay, which is something I could never bring up to Ma or Pa. They wouldn't understand. They would probably disown me. So, I definitely won't be telling them I like Carl anytime soon, or maybe, ever. But I kind of do want to tell Carl. I think I'll wait for when the time is right. We're hanging out again tomorrow, to actually do homework this time.

It's kind of late, so I think I'm going to shower and get ready for bed. Talk to you tomorrow, Journal!!

March 4th

I'm a bit confused, kind of sad, a smidge exhausted, and just very emotionally depleted right now.

I don't really know where to start, so I guess I'll start with this morning. I did a full practice exam for the SAT before school, and my score was actually a lot better than I thought it would be. If I can manage to get a similar score, but hopefully better, on the real exam, I think I could get into a lot of the schools I've had my eye on, maybe even a school that's a tier up.

That was pretty much as good as my day got. Actually, no. I need to stop wallowing and being so overdramatic. My day wasn't great, but it wasn't terrible. I am 100 percent positive that there are many, many people whose day was worse than mine. Also many people whose day was better. I mean, there is someone out there who won the lottery today, but then again, there is also someone out there whose mom died today. So I guess, in the context of the greater world, my day wasn't as bad as it could have been.

I'm just going to cut to the chase. I knew I said I was going to wait for the right time, but I have the patience of a literal five-year-old, so that didn't happen. I told Carl that I liked him. He was confused. I explained to him that I meant as more than a friend. He got awkward. Tried to treat me like a bro. I got awkward. We drove in silence. He dropped me home. Not sure if I'll ever see him again. FML. LOL. This. Sucks.

At least I don't have to tell Ma and Pa anything. And maybe I'm not gay. Maybe I didn't even really like Carl but was just confused. I've just got a lot of thoughts right now, and I don't even know how to process them. Literally everything I wrote in the last sentence was a lie. I mean, deep down I know that. I'm not straight. I did like Carl. I *do* like Carl. But it would just be easier to pretend if I didn't, you know? I wouldn't have to deal with these feelings. Ugh, feelings.

I feel like…I don't even know what I feel. Cara's crying in the other room, so I'll go check on her and then come back.

"I believe in the fire of love and the sweat of truth."
—ASSATA SHAKUR

IRIS

―

I tie my hair back into a ponytail, unsticking it from the sweat on my neck. The air is hot and sticky, but the occasional breeze makes it a bit more bearable. I've heard of Iris's name in passing, but have never actually met her. She graduated from a university not too far from my own.

Initially, when she told me to meet her on the roof of the library, I was a bit worried. Being on the roofs of buildings is almost always restricted access, but she assured me that this roof was different, and it was. It was designed to be explored by students and travelers alike. The skyline of the city is visible in one section of the roof patio, while trees and plants adorn the rest of it.

Not entirely sure where to wait for Iris, I kind of just sit on the steps, visible from the entrance of the roof. Iris brings her own energy. Even though I've only communicated with her through a few emails and a couple texts, there is no doubt in my mind that this is her. With her carefree aura, we settle into easy conversation. She tells me about being back on campus and how it feels.

It's been a really long while since I've been back here. Which is quite odd, considering I work at a coffeeshop that is not even a block away. The open air of the roof is a sharp contrast of the building that sits beneath it. As a student, I spent almost every night in this library. It wasn't until the end of my second year that I realized what a haven this rooftop offers students.

The views are breathtaking at every time of the day. I think the best view of the skyline of the city is best seen from that nestled corner, especially as the sun sets.

She points to the corner of the roof I first noticed when I arrived. She's right, the views are really quite stunning. I can't even imagine what a sunset would look like from here.

The triangular glass prisms reflect the colors of the sky at the break of dawn and as dusk settles. Right before my last finals period senior year, my friend and I watched the sunset from this same rooftop and then headed to the basement of the library to prep for our impending computer science exam the next day. Less than twelve hours after, we came back up to the same spot and watched the sunrise. A new day had begun.

I remember having a similar night. I think it's easier for ten-minute study breaks to turn into four-hour life breaks when a major test or assignment looms over your head for the next morning.

As the dark night turned to day, after hours of studying but mostly talking, we abandoned our books when the sun said hello. Rays of sunshine peeked through the windows of the room we had set up camp in for the night. Both of us quickly hit Save on the Word documents we had been working on on our computers, shoved everything from the table into our backpacks, and hurried outside to catch the sun rising in the distance.

I don't remember what I got on that exam; I don't even remember if I did well or not. I do remember sitting with him and talking about absolutely everything and absolutely nothing for hours. We talked about how he drinks his coffee black, but only if it's cold outside. We wondered where Malala Yousafzai got her strength from and how she continues to fight on. We debated whether there was life beyond just this planet—I definitely think there is. I think we also may have watched a few too many Vine compilation videos on YouTube.

That was only one of many nights I spent on this campus feeling incredibly grateful for the new life this ivory tower had given me, which is a pretty conflicting thought to have.

When I was back home in high school, my mother and father, even I, didn't think that I would be able to get to America, the alleged land of great opportunity. After being on the visa waitlist for more than our patience allowed, my father suggested I look at universities in the United States and apply for a student visa rather than a tourist visa. While I had always considered it in the back of my mind, I was insistent on studying in the UK. Tuition was significantly less, and I would receive a comparable education in regards to both content and prestige.

In total, I applied to seven universities. Six in the United Kingdom and one in America.

I told myself—pretty willfully too—that I wouldn't go to the United States for education unless I could find some miraculous scholarships that would help reduce the cost so that my parents wouldn't have to provide a significant contribution, even though I knew that they would've given up everything for my education in a heartbeat. I just didn't want the prospect of a diploma, of a single piece of fancy paper, uprooting their entire livelihoods.

Although, even now, standing on the other side with that fancy paper in hand (or rather, collecting dust somewhere in my basement), I'm not sure it was worth all the hype. The experience of going to university was. But the paper itself? I'm just not so sure.

There were many nights I spent in the library, texting group messages to friends asking if any of them had a charger for my dying devices. We rewarded ourselves with incremental coffee breaks that sometimes ended up lasting far longer than our study sessions did altogether.

I knew my friends' drink orders by heart. I still do. I always settled for chamomile tea, though. Even now, working at a coffeeshop, I'm just not much of a java person. Studying while in uni is quite an experience. Within the walls of the library, there are hundreds of stressed-out students all studying different subjects through different assignments on different timelines, yet they are mutually suffering together.

As late as my nights were at the library, they were early at the engineering complex. By no means did I make it to my morning classes on time every day, but I did try. Granted, the days I would have made it there with time to spare, I usually stopped to get a blueberry muffin. Looking back, I'm glad that I even stopped to warm it up, sacrificing a minute of instruction for the warmth of the sweet bread to make my morning all that much better.

I liked the classroom buildings the most in the early mornings, though, that is, the few times I was up early enough to see them empty. It's interesting how the walls hold so many stories. I feel like you can really tell that when they aren't crammed with kids.

I've never really heard walls speak any stories to me, but with the amount of unique students from so many different walks of life who pass through every day and every year, I'm sure that they've seen and heard more than they get credit for.

I completely understand stopping for the morning breakfast, though. My go-to is an everything bagel with cream cheese.

As much as I loved going to classes where I felt inspired, where I felt like I was actually learning, my university experience was far from perfect. While I wish every class made me excited, I think throughout my entire four-year/eight-semester career, there were only two of those.

Only two. That's absolutely wild.

Coming into university, I thought every class would blow my mind and every professor I had would inspire me to see the world in a new light. I imagined I would walk across the quad with my professor pondering the multiplex of human organisms and their complexities with the environments around them, like a scene straight out of *A Beautiful Mind*.

But instead, I ended up contemplating if I should drop not just my major, but out of university altogether, many times in the dining hall. Instead of being like the genius of Matt Damon's character from *Good Will Hunting*, I ended up many times in a chair outside of my professor's office bursting into tears. Once, even inside her office.

Knowing that Iris, with all her sporadic energy and carefree will, has cried in front of her professor during office hours is somehow very comforting to me. I had done the same, almost. It wasn't a professor but the head of the study abroad program at the beginning of the semester. What a rough start.

I found myself thrust into a new environment that was completely different from what I could have possibly expected, regardless of how many YouTube videos and vlogs I watched in preparation. On the academic side, I found myself sitting in classes, feeling indifferent about the course material.

I'd never fallen asleep in high school or let myself get distracted by my phone during class, something I took great pride in. But in my first full month of university classes, I had managed to do both. I was now one of those kids who surfed Facebook on their laptop and watched episodes of *The Bachelor* muted with subtitles. It was easy to become someone that I had for so long tried not to become.

Emotionally, it was hard to connect with people who could drive home on the weekends to get a quick meal with their family, when I hadn't talked to my parents in weeks. Having roommates saved me in more ways than I can ever think possible. Adjusting to sharing my space with two other completely random human beings was not easy at first, or ever. Actually, it gave me people to find comfort in.

We get up from our spot on the roof as a college-aged tour guide comes by with a group of prospective students, pointing out the views we've been mesmerized by for the past half an hour. Iris keeps talking as we walk through the academic quad. She points out the different buildings, one home to the Economics department, another for the Political Science and International Relations ones. The green grass has been meticulously cut, not a weed in sight. At the end of the quad is a large statue of the university's mascot. It's not hard to tell that it is most definitely a tourist stop for pictures.

Our minifridge was equally sectioned off in thirds, clearly marked with washi tape lines. Yet, I still found that sometimes my string cheese would go missing and the convicting wrappers could be found at the foot of one of my roommate's beds. Between the three of us, our room always inevitably had an abundance of hair everywhere: in the carpet, near the mirror, on the sheets, just, everywhere. But between the three of us, our room also always inevitably had an abundance of love everywhere: the good luck post-it notes on exam days, the "I'm sorry for being so loud last night" cookies, and the medicinal supply and mothering ways that would appear when one of us fell sick.

Coming home after a bad test, knowing that two hugs would be waiting for me, made it worth the nights I got restless sleep because someone was talking on the phone a little too loud or the days when there was mold in the fridge because someone forgot to throw out the milk. The endless weeks of movie nights, Netflix binges, many pints of Ben and Jerry's Chunky Monkey ice cream, impromptu dance parties, as fun as they were, only contributed to the bubble I spent those four years in.

The real world is different. Much harder. Much tougher. Just, much more real.

Having two roommates must have been like living in eternal chaos. Even with just one roommate, I found the room a bit too small some nights. But having a roommate makes the college experience better. Well, I guess if you are lucky enough to have a compatible roommate.

Until my second year of college, I had never really shared my room or my space with another person. But on move-in day, I had to learn very quickly. Everything on my roommate's side of the room, I could see, and she could do the same for everything on my side. If I leaned far enough over, I could touch her bed. That's how small our room was.

Before the winter set in, the room always seemed way too small and way too stuffy. There was no air conditioning, and the body heat of even one more person often made me feel like I was sitting in an oven. But as the temperature cooled down, so did we. I don't think I would have the same friends or memories if I hadn't met my roommate, or even more so, if I hadn't been friends with her.

We paid rent and utilities when we lived off campus in university. Our landlord would come on the first of every month at exactly 7:24 a.m. to collect it. She was a strange woman. But now, it's my responsibility to send off that rent check to the managing company.

Two months ago, I wrote the check, signed it, dated it, did everything. I put the check in an envelope, addressed it, wrote my return address, sealed it, mailed it, took a deep breath, you know. Four days later, I got a message from the leasing office saying they hadn't received my rent check. I got home to the same envelope sitting in my mailbox. I had forgotten to put a stamp on it.

The real world also doesn't come with spending on my parents' dime or unlimited meal plans. Cereal and, as basic as it sounds, avocado toast are honestly my fallback dishes. Rice and beans too. They come in a can and are easy enough to pour out and warm up.

University spoiled me, but don't get me wrong, I learned quite a bit too.

The communal restrooms taught me the importance of shower shoes. The dining halls taught me how to create makeshift containers out of paper napkins to maximize the amount of snacks I could steal from them. I learned how to pack very quick impromptu picnic baskets for dinner on the lawn when the sky looked like the sunset was going to be especially beautiful that evening. Tuesday evenings taught me to never make plans because I always had a club meeting on the third floor of the English department building. I learned the best way to gain both traction and speed when sledding down the hill with dining trays on snow days.

I learned a lot from my four years here. But I learned more from the people than I ever did the institution.

We walk down a hill of stairs to a small bakery. The overwhelming smell of croissants and coffee envelope me. We sit at a table by the windows, waiting for our order, as Iris keeps talking. I take out my notebook again and continue to record her thoughts.

My citizenship status was, I suppose, a conscious decision on my part, though. After I graduated, I couldn't find a job that was willing to sponsor my visa. So I booked a flight home. I just didn't get on it. My student visa had expired, but I was still living in the United States.

I found a job at the coffeeshop right down the street. It's a really popular place for most of the students on campus to hang out and study. We're always pretty busy. I remember my first year of university, my first date was actually at the same coffeeshop. I ordered a pastry and a coffee, which at the time, I found way too strong but pretended to love and drank anyways.

How long has it been since she's seen her parents? Her family? Did they encourage her to outstay her visa, or did she do it on her own?

Even now, my friends and coworkers, many of them don't know that I'm undocumented. They just think I'm an international student who graduated. Actually, I'm not sure they even think about my visa status, or nonstatus, for that matter. Telling the people I'm close to that I'm undocumented would either change their perception of me or put my safety at risk, and I'm not really willing to take a chance on either of those.

And it's not like I didn't try to go through the process. I did. I'm not sure how outright I have to be, but obviously I don't want to be undocumented. There's too many barriers, too much uncertainty.

Applying for a different type of visa without job sponsorship was too much of a gamble. I wasn't eligible for CPT, which is a curricular training program that allows students with F-1 visas to work, because it must be completed before graduation. Similarly, with the OPT, or Optional Program Training, you have to have a valid F-1 visa, and mine expired with my graduation, or a couple weeks after, actually.

Many people apply for extensions on their F-1 visa and then apply for OPT, which lets them stay for up to almost two years after graduating to work, but you have to have a job lined up that is willing to work with your immigration status, and it must be kind of related to what you studied in college, or at least be an application of those studies.

I could have also applied for the H-1B visa status had I gotten on that plane home and then tried to come back. But that was the scary part: What if I wasn't allowed back? This small city is my life now. This community has given a lot to me, but I've also given a lot to this community too.

I'm still in my midtwenties, but I'm not really sure what to do from here. I've been thinking about that a lot lately. As much as I love the coffeeshop, I don't want to work there for the rest of my life. I have a world class education and skills that I know I can utilize to do something a little more important.

I guess I should also be a bit more clear. To me, I'm still not sure if the college degree was worth it. The more I think about it, the less I believe it was. To get a single piece of paper, I had to pay so much, take so many classes that I didn't really enjoy but just to fulfill requirements, and then on top of that, jump through hoops and obstacles to petition getting my degree on time. That's a whole other story with my thesis and making sure it counted for credit. It was a mess.

But the paper is important. I don't think there's many jobs that I would be eligible for without a bachelor's. And with the way we're headed, probably even a master's degree. This is good, though. It's good that more education is becoming the norm. But attending a four year university is not the only way to get an education. It may be the most "traditional" way, but by no means is it the best. I mean, there's just too many barriers, largely the financial aspect of rising tuition rates, especially for private colleges.

But I do think that the university *experience* was worth it, and I would do it a million times again if I was ever asked. I'm very conflicted about the idea of a college education, but it's an opportunity and a privilege to be able to go, which is why I really do value the time I spent here. But also, education shouldn't have to be a privilege. It should be a right. See? It's causes some very conflicting feelings. Anyway, I digress.

Now, it's either finding a country that I want to live in that will take me or getting deported and going home. I guess I could also marry a US citizen and apply that way, but I don't want to get married for the wrong reasons. I mean, my mom would love to see me get married.

I haven't seen her in a while, since graduation. I FaceTimed her and my dad the other day. After so many years, they still don't really understand they should hold the phone camera out straight instead of under their chins to look down on it. I call home every once in a while now, to make sure that they're doing all right. Even halfway across the world, so many years later, they are everything that I have and everything that I am.

I smile, thinking of my own parents and their mutual inability to properly participate in a FaceTime call.

Regardless of what my parents think, and what my mom wants, I'm not going to marry for citizenship. Because love will come, at least I hope it will. So, why rush it?

With that, Iris is done. I thank her for her time, and she thanks me for mine. I take our dishes to the rack and wave

Iris goodbye, grabbing my notebook and backpack on my way out. Isn't it a bit ironic how the one who was the most excited about studying in the US has become the most cynical?

Iris is a college-educated woman who fulfilled all of her requirements, was granted the degree, and yet, she still doesn't believe in the paper itself.

"Forgiveness and faith are like writing a story. They take time, effort, revisions."
—DAISY HERNANDEZ

AKINA AND AIDEE

My little sister's name is Akina. While I wish this was my story to tell, it's not. It's really her story. This is Akina's world, and we are all just living in it.

My name means "helper" or "aid," but Akina means "solidarity" in Swahili. While some may say she was a miracle for my parents and my family, I think she was fate. Not destiny, which I believe can be shaped by one's actions, but fate, which is only in the hands of a higher power. Akina is what kept our family from falling apart at the time, but even today she is my strength, my rock, in every sense of the word.

With a head of curly, dark, usually tangled, hair and an infectious smile, Akina is hard to miss in a crowd. She brings light with her wherever she goes and has this innate ability to be exactly what a person is looking for and say exactly what they are hoping for. And, she's not even five years old yet. (If Akina could understand what I was writing, she would correct me to say that she is actually four years and seven and a half months old.)

While our names are of Swahili origins, we are far from the subcontinent of our original brothers and sisters. (My mom named both of us. She chose Swahili names because while she had never been to Africa, she always said she felt a strong connection to the continent.) I grew up in an area of Tijuana, Mexico, that borders the United States. Akina is still growing up, but I hope when she is older and people ask her where she grew up, she can say the United States.

Right now, Akina is napping, which doesn't happen very frequently. It's hard to keep up with all her energy, and I truly do not know where she gets it all from. Definitely not the food, because we just don't have enough of it. I braided her hair back this morning, but even so, her curls are everywhere because they truly just cannot be tamed. Her head is in my lap, and her small body is strewn across our few belongings—my backpack, a small sleeping bag, and a water canteen that is bordering on empty. We'll start rationing soon, though.

We are still waiting at the border checkpoint. It's been a couple days now, but hopefully we will hear our names called soon. When I went to write our names in the book to seek asylum in the United States, I wrote that Akina was my daughter. She is only ten years younger than me, but hopefully I look older than I am and no one will notice. Children aren't allowed to put their name in the book. There are organizations that help kids claim asylum, but all of them are incredibly overwhelmed and backed up.

I didn't want to take a chance with Akina. I had to get her out before more changes happen. I feel as though almost every day there are changes happening, and not good ones. Changes enacted by presidents and people in power who don't know what it is like to live the way the majority of the country lives, as part of the working class. There's too many people in charge who don't think about the effect that their words can have on the entire lives of others, people who wouldn't last a day living the way Akina and I do.

There are many people waiting with us. At least a thousand, I can be sure. Actually, not entirely sure, but pretty confident. Waiting here at the border, there is a strange sense of vulnerability. These thousand or so people who are sitting here and waiting just like us are strangers, but strangers who have, at least in some way, walked a similar path to me.

While I should not make assumptions, I know that these people are hoping to seek refuge in the United States, likely to escape the gang violence and cartels that have started to take over our small hometowns. This should unite us. We suffered together, and we are trying to leave together. But it's also very isolating. When another family's name gets called, I want to be happy for them. They have the opportunity to start a new life, but I find myself envious and, in part, angry that it wasn't my name called.

It's also hard to hear a whole family's name called because I not only wish that was me, but I wish that was my full nuclear family. I love being with Akina, but it's hard. I feel like I have to not only be a brother to her but a mother and father too. Mom and Dad were good parents. I still think they are, wherever they are. They're just not good parents to us anymore.

When I was younger, we had a lot of family traditions. We would paint small dreidels together and make potato latkes before Hanukkah. We aren't Jewish. We would fast together during Ramadan and celebrate Eid with sweet rice pudding. We aren't Muslim. We would choose something to give up during Lent and would go to church on Christmas Eve. We aren't Christian. It wasn't just religious traditions we celebrated. We also threw colors at each other for Holi, visited the gravesites of deceased family members for Día de los Muertos, and released lanterns on the Chinese New Year. My parents had an appreciation for other cultures and religions that many people don't have.

Their open-mindedness is why I was so shocked when I heard the alleged true story of what happened to them. I know that this is a true story and that I should believe it, but there is this small part of me that doesn't want to believe it. I knew that my parents were outspoken advocates against the gangs. I always feared for them but knew that they were smart enough to be careful enough to protect our family.

Mom and Dad were the dream team. I don't think I will ever meet another set of people who are so in sync with each other, who are always on the same page, who were quite literally the same soul, just in two separate bodies.

I don't exactly remember the day. I've tried pretty hard to forget it, actually. I remember picking up Akina from day care on the way home from school. I would pick her up every day because it was on the way home. Mom would drop her off, though, because the day care classes started later than I liked to get to school. I remember it was a Thursday, and I only remember that because the night market is closed on Thursdays, and that night it was closed. When Akina and I got home, neither Mom nor Dad were there, and usually at least one of them is.

I made grilled cheese and tortilla wraps for Akina, and then I set her up with her practice pebbles to learn how to count. I sat down across from her to do my own homework. I think around when the sun started to set, I started to get worried because Mom and Dad still weren't home.

We weren't really wealthy, but cellphones were a thing. I didn't have one, but Mom and Dad did. I was in seventh grade at the time. I went over to the Salinas' house to see if one of them would be able to call Mom or Dad to see if they were getting held up or just to make sure everything was okay.

I left Akina in the house, which I now realize was a stupid decision. She was taking a nap, and like I mentioned before, she doesn't do that very often. I went over, and Mrs. Salinas let me use their phone to call. I tried both numbers a couple times, but they didn't go through.

Mrs. Salinas told me to go fetch Akina and for us to stay in their home until Mom or Dad came home so that we were safe. The Salinases have twin boys, both of which had been deployed with the Mexican Army for a couple months at the time. I think it was around midnight when Mr. Salinas went over to the Despedidas' house to ask if they knew where Mom and Dad had been held up.

Mr. Despedida had apparently been knocking on our door to get ahold of me to check on Akina and I. He didn't have much information, but said that Mom and Dad had been picked up by some not-so-good people. I remember being so frustrated and angry at them. I was convinced that it was because they would set up these rallies and protests speaking out against the government. It was why Akina and I would be without parents that night.

One night without parents turned into three years since. They never came back home or contacted us. We spent the first couple weeks with the Salinases and then the next couple with the Despedidas and then the next couple with the Santoses.

At that point, it had been almost three months and the constant movement was getting exhausting. Akina and I moved back into our house, but the neighborhood still took care of us. Mr. Salinas taught me how to use less electricity so we could pay for the bills with what money Mom and Dad had kept in the armoire. I started working at the convenient store a couple blocks over. I learned how to cook too.

Every once in a while, someone would bring over warm tamales or some fresh pico de gallo, which Akina and I both really appreciated. Eventually, though, it was just too much. I didn't like living in the house that we used to do all these traditions in and celebrate all these festivities with Mom and Dad, without them.

I thought about leaving, a lot. But never thought about it too seriously. I think I was hoping that one day while

Akina was drawing after dinner and I was doing my homework, Mom and Dad would come through the front door, hugging us to make up for lost time and explaining what had happened. That was the fairytale I'd daydream about while working shifts at the convenient store. But that's all it was: a fairy tale.

The breaking point, I guess some would call it, was when Mr. Despedida came over one evening after Akina had already gone to bed. He told me that Mom and Dad hadn't gotten arrested for speaking out. I was obviously confused. He explained to me how they had been working with one of the cartels, selling, shipping, and trading drugs. He found this out from a friend's brother's wife who worked with someone somewhere. I just didn't really believe it at first but also because I just didn't really understand it. I still don't.

Mr. Despedida didn't know if they had been picked up by their own cartel with the intention that they would be full-time dealers (kids are too much of a liability), or if they had been caught and arrested. As bad as it sounds, I hope it was the former. Being arrested means life in prison, which in Mexico is worse than death itself.

I just hope that they come back, with a good excuse and a corroborated story, before Akina is old enough and I have to be the one to explain to her that the reason we are camped out at the border is to escape an environment that, in part, exists because of people like Mom and Dad.

It's just Akina is such a pure soul. While I have every reason to be biased, I don't think I'm unjustified in truly believing that she is different. Akina has an awareness for the world around her and a genuine love for the humans around her. Maybe I am too much of a cynic already, maybe she's young and naive, but I think that Akina chooses to see the best in people, and that's something I don't think I want to see change.

I run my hand through her messy curls as she stirs in her sleep. The sun is just rising now, yellows and oranges streaking the sky in the distance. It looks like the world is on fire and still burning. It kind of feels like that too.

Guards patrol the fence, canines sniffing around. The notebook guardian opens the book and begins calling names. I'm hoping our name will be called soon, but to be frank, I'm not sure what to do when it is.

Cross the border, go to America with what little money I have saved, and do what? Go where?

Staying home meant being unsafe, but going to America, there's so many unknowns. Maybe going back to our small home, using less and less electricity and working in the convenience store, is the better idea. There, we have a whole village looking after us. When our name gets called, we go to America, and do what? I will always look after Akina, but who will look after me? Our English is broken, we don't have much money, and we don't know anyone on the other side of this intimidating fence. I think the idea of starting over seems better on paper than it does in real life right now.

As Akina wakes, she asks if our name will be called today. This is the first thing she asks every morning. Before I get the chance to respond, the guardian of the notebook calls out:

"Aidee and Akina Caraballo-Sotomayor."

* * *

The Los Angeles Times has named Tijuana, Mexico, "one of the deadliest cities in the world" after a record number of killings in 2018: 2,518 people, a number almost seven times the total in 2012. Tijuana has a rate of 140 killings per 100,000 people (for reference, just across the border from Tijuana, San Diego has a rate of approximately 2 killings per 100,000 people).

The rising number of homicides has been largely attributed to the rapid spread of methamphetamine, or crystal, on the streets of Tijuana. The dealing of crystal by thousands of competing gangs has been observed in both the slums and wealthier neighborhoods alike. Competition to sell between gangs has led to spikes in rates of both addiction and violence.

citations: https://www.latimes.com/local/california/la-me-asylum-seekers-notebook-holds-key-to-entry-20180705-story.html & https://www.latimes.com/world/mexico-americas/la-fg-mexico-tijuana-drug-violence-20190130-htmlstory.html

"Love recognizes no barriers. It jumps hurdles, leaps fences, penetrates walls to arrive at its destination full of hope."

—MAYA ANGELOU

EPILOGUE

You've read these stories, but know that there are millions more that are like them, and different, all at the same time.

Undocumented immigration is often deeply politicized in our world, as we see the rise of instantaneous media and socialization; it is often a buzzword phrase used on the scrolling banners at the bottom of Fox News broadcasts and as the captions of clickbait articles on Facebook. But what these news clips and articles often fail to show is the people behind these headlines.

The people behind these stories are *real*.

Over the past year, I have had the chance to meet the people in these stories and hear their journeys. In learning about them, where they come from and their trials and tribulations, I've also learned a lot about myself, who I am and who I want to be.

The most important thing I've learned is that these individuals are like you and they're like me. These people not only live in our communities but they are often the ones who help build them and the ones who help them thrive. These people are the ones who play with us on our soccer teams, the ones who study beside us in the library, the ones who help stock our grocery stores in the middle of the night, the ones who know our drink orders the minute we walk into our favorite coffeeshops, the ones who are studying to be doctors and artists, just like we dream to be.

We share dreams and we share hope, hope for a better future, for a better tomorrow, and for a better world.

It is our collective responsibility to be open-minded, to be welcoming and inclusive, to hear the stories, the struggles, and the successes of our fellow humans. It is important that we put humanity, compassion, and love for others before politics, and it is important that we do this now because these are the stories of the past, the stories of today, and the stories of tomorrow. These are the stories of us.

"Make a difference about something other than yourselves."
—TONI MORRISON

RESOURCES & NEXT STEPS

Hopefully, after reading the stories of Aury, Pablito, Emily, Sahara, Donavan, Paola, Kabira, Iris, Aidee, and Akina, you want to learn more and take action. In the following pages are some resources, which include organizations that are actively working both on the ground and on the legislative level to advocate for the rights of immigrants who are currently living or coming into the United States. I hope that you look to these organizations with the aspirations of simply learning more, donating, volunteering, or getting involved in any way that best suits you.

TEXAS CIVIL RIGHTS PROJECT

"The Texas Civil Rights Project is fighting around the clock to reunite the 382 families they represent and to ensure that they get excellent legal representation on their underlying immigration claims.

They will continue to go to court every day in South Texas to monitor and protect against the ever-changing policies of the Trump Administration for as long as it is necessary. Their lawyers are working to stop family separation permanently in an action against the United States before an international human rights body called the Inter-American Commission on Human Rights.

At the same time, they are working hand-in-hand with partners across Texas and the country to end the Zero Tolerance policy and ensure that no human rights or civil rights violations at the border these past weeks are allowed to continue, resume, or take place ever again."

Learn more at www.texascivilrightsproject.org.

THE REFUGEE AND IMMIGRANT CENTER FOR EDUCATION AND LEGAL SERVICES

"The Refugee and Immigrant Center for Education and Legal Services (RAICES) is a nonprofit agency that promotes justice *by providing free and low-cost legal services to underserved immigrant children, families, and refugees.*

A diverse staff of 130 attorneys, legal assistants, and support staff provide consultations, direct legal services, representation, assistance, and advocacy to communities in Texas and to clients after they leave the state. In 2017, RAICES staff closed fifty-one thousand cases at no cost to the client.

Their advocacy and commitment to change are driven by the clients and families they serve every day as their attorneys and legal assistants provide legal advocacy and representation in an immigration system that breaks apart families and leaves millions without pathways to legal status."

Learn more at www.raicestexas.org.

THE AMERICAN CIVIL LIBERTIES UNION

"The American Civil Liberties Union (ACLU) actively works to defend the civil liberties and rights of American citizens, including the rights of immigrants who seek asylum in the United States to escape persecution from other countries.

They work to change policy as well as hearts and minds. Their Washington Legislative Office lobbies Congress to pass bills that advance or defend civil liberties and defeat those that do not, their affiliates work in state houses across the country to do the same, and they use strategic communications to engage supporters on the most pressing civil liberties issues of our time."

Learn more at www.aclu.org.

THE FLORENCE PROJECT

"The Florence Project is a nonprofit legal service organization providing free legal and social services to adults and unaccompanied children in immigration custody in Arizona. Although the government assists indigent criminal defendants and civil litigants through public defenders and legal aid attorneys, it does not provide attorneys for people in immigration removal proceedings.

As a result, an estimated 86 percent of detained people go unrepresented due to poverty. The Florence Project strives to address this inequity both locally and nationally through direct service, partnerships with the community, and advocacy and outreach efforts."

Learn more at www.firrp.org.

UNITED WE DREAM

"United We Dream is the largest immigrant youth-led community in the country. They create welcoming spaces for young people—regardless of immigration status—to support, engage, and empower them to make their voice heard and win. They have an online reach of over 4 million and are made up of over 400,000 members as well as five statewide branches and over 100 local groups across 28 states. Over 60 percent of their members are women, and 20 percent identify as LGBTQ.

Whether they're organizing in the streets, building cutting-edge technology systems, opening doors for LGBTQ immigrant youth, clearing pathways to education, stopping deportations or creating alliances across social movements, United We Dream puts undocumented immigrant youth in the driver's seat to strategize, innovate, and win."

Learn more at www.unitedwedream.org.

"No tree survives alone in the forest."

—BRIT MARLING, *THE OA*

ACKNOWLEDGMENTS

I have the absolute best human beings in my corner, and for that I could not be more grateful.

Mom and Dad, for giving me the world. For the late nights, the early mornings, the drives to school (which eventually became flights), for always having faith in me, encouraging me to keep following (and finding) new passions, for always, always being my biggest supporters.

Sara and Zoya, both of you inspire me each and every day in so many different ways. Sara, you inspire me to want to keep reading and to want to keep learning. The fact that you do so much with a (mostly) positive attitude blows me away every time I think about it. Zo, your sheer willingness to stand up for yourself and others (and also not taking shiz from anyone else— kind of good scary sometimes) encourages me to want to do the same. You both are my absolute world, from fighting in the back seat of Mom's car when I ripped up your UNO cards to sitting in Sara's closet eating beef jerky in Corpus to under the Northern Lights in Iceland, to everywhere we've been and everywhere we still have yet to go.

To my dada, I love you more than words could ever explain. Your weekly phone calls, secret recipe French toast, and love for all things dessert make me so proud to be your granddaughter.

To my family, my cousins and aunts and uncles and grandparents, both near and far, thank you for inspiring me to want to be the best version of myself and for giving me more love and support than I could have ever asked for.

To the very best friends anyone could ever ask for, thank you a trillion times over.

Lulu Soghaier, from forcing you not to drop out of our first semester ExCollege course to having the chance to teach our own, from Facebook baby meme tags (tatummmm) to streaming episodes of our favorite Hulu shows with Takis in hand, from Corpus visits to fudgy Carm brownies, from bad Photoshops to endless sushi, you are my rock.

Cansu Gundem, for endless Tisch selfies, brushing our teeth and sink spitting, never saying no to watching another vine compilation, minion girl, mascara tears in Carm, and talking through our existential crisis together, from Capen to tie-dye drinks in unnamed hotel cafés, your friendship means so much to me.

Gabrielle De Weck, for decorating for the holidays to awkwardly leaving restaurants, for killing it at Joshua's trivia night to getting hangry in D.C., for trillers in our new home, trying not to turn into subletters, our honeymoon bathroom, and corner bedrooms, there's no one I rather be forever next-door neighbors with.

Deeya Shroff, for making me laugh more than you'll ever know, for our first of (hopefully) many gospel choir semesters together, arachnids, sriracha salads, jojoba nails, decorating elephant cookies (even though mine was better), *the* leggings, for always giving it to me straight, and for always believing in me.

Lal Kokoglu, for deep-end chocolate chip cookies, eyebrow plucks, impromptu dance parties, copying what I wear, literally endless chewing gum, Gerber baby tears, and loving Noah Ritter as much as I do, there's not a greater fr or oomie in this world.

Anila Katragadda, you are my all-time forever friend and soul sister. From fractured skulls to bloody ears, secrets I'll keep forever and pacts I'll never break, I love you forever and ever.

Akshat Rajan, for binge watching *Designated Survivor*, Mathilda and the birthday cake, sunrises from Eaton, t jeff, TEDx, and never letting me actually cut your hair (honestly, a very good call), thank you for pushing me to trust the unknown.

Jordan Moeller, from a switch into Cissy's class to Mr. Jesse's banana surgery, from all of my coronets proposals to our fish friend, a friendship made in Baker that has far outlived that. It's your turn to visit now!

Aleena Villareal, for kazoozles behind the tribunal desk to Nutella popcorn, early mornings with iConquer to the My Favorite Muffins that followed, from snail mail letters to secret code words, Julia Pastrana projects to dolphin jumping pictures, I love you so much.

Ventura Lopez, Hunter Saenz, Jasbeth DeLaRosa, Katherine Krockover, Andrew Leeton and Karla Alaniz, for food hops and Sno-Balls, Ocean Drive cruises, attempted sunrises, pep rallies to prom, baking brownies to board game nights, thank you for being the reason that I call Corpus home.

Thalia Trentacarlini, for being the most encouraging, most real, most trusting person I have ever known. From sunrise to Chapman's Peak, Los Angeles to Boston, swinging ponytails to baking cake with Adil, ringworm to Blue Bird spicy chicken to chocolate cake at Xpressions, I am so grateful for you.

To the amazing team at New Degree Press, Eric Koester, Cass Lauer, Kristy Carter, and Brian Bies, thank you for supporting me, encouraging me, and for believing in me and my ideas.

To Gabrielle Lencioni, Ava Soltani, Sophia Papakostas, Josh Kaplan, Valeria Lopez, Muhammad Patel, Emily Moravits, Abigail Cieslik, Augusta Koelsch, Kately Pieper, Karen Case, Emma Gordon, Fredel Cohen, Emily Auton, Natasha Valrani, Mahima Agarwal, Holly Zhang, Ronnie Marie Falasco, Julie Chen, Lucia Boyd, Yara El-Khatib, Sravya Alla, Melissa Wood, Julie Manuszak, Shefali Dahiya, Kate Canavan, Lucy Hotz, my TEDxTufts, TUSC, Chi Omega and Coca-Cola Scholar families, and all the friendships I have made through Windsor Park, Baker, Carroll, Veterans Memorial, and Tufts for being a beacon of light in my life and a constant source of never-ending love and support.

To my friendtors: Mary Pat McMahon, Pratap Misra, Kate Drizos Cavell, Samuel Sommers, Henry De Sio, Jeff Berry, John Wescott, Maria Champlin, Shaashi Singh, Nina Drath, Randi Jones, Kim James, Marsha Hutchens, Velia Zamora, Roland Hernandez, Daniel Garza, Jenifer Martinez, Sydna Arnold, Cissy Smith, Gary Henicke, Melinda Ramirez, Coleton Whitaker, Anthony Lamorena, and all the wonderful people I had the chance to work with at Quorum and in Muizenberg, I look up to you and am forever thankful for all that you have taught me and continue to teach me.

Lastly, I want to thank *you* for reading along, supporting me, and helping give these incredible people a platform through which they can share their powerful stories. The world is a better place with people who are willing to listen and learn, so for that, I thank you with all my heart.

"Sometimes the most healing thing to do is remind ourselves over and over and over, other people feel this too."
—ANDREA GIBSON

CPSIA information can be obtained
at www.ICGtesting.com
Printed in the USA
FSHW011826261119
64499FS